Revolution *of* Character

Dallas Willard
with
Don Simpson

Revolution *of* Character

DISCOVERING CHRIST'S PATTERN
for SPIRITUAL TRANSFORMATION

NAVPRESS®

BRINGING TRUTH TO LIFE

OUR GUARANTEE TO YOU

We believe so strongly in the message of our books that we are making this quality guarantee to you. If for any reason you are disappointed with the content of this book, return the title page to us with your name and address and we will refund to you the list price of the book. To help us serve you better, please briefly describe why you were disappointed. Mail your refund request to: NavPress, P.O. Box 35002, Colorado Springs, CO 80935.

The Navigators is an international Christian organization. Our mission is to reach, disciple, and equip people to know Christ and to make Him known through successive generations. We envision multitudes of diverse people in the United States and every other nation who have a passionate love for Christ, live a lifestyle of sharing Christ's love, and multiply spiritual laborers among those without Christ.

NavPress is the publishing ministry of The Navigators. NavPress publications help believers learn biblical truth and apply what they learn to their lives and ministries. Our mission is to stimulate spiritual formation among our readers.

ISBN 1-57683-857-9

Cover design by StudioGearbox
Cover photo by Neo Vision/Photonica
Creative Team: Don Simpson, Karen Lee-Thorp, Arvid Wallen, Kathy Mosier, Glynese Northam

Some of the anecdotal illustrations in this book are true to life and are included with the permission of the persons involved. All other illustrations are composites of real situations, and any resemblance to people living or dead is coincidental.

Unless otherwise identified, all Scripture quotations in this publication are taken from the *New American Standard Bible* (NASB), © The Lockman Foundation 1960, 1962, 1963, 1968, 1971, 1972, 1973, 1975, 1977, 1995. The author's paraphrases and translations are marked as PAR. Other versions used include the HOLY BIBLE: NEW INTERNATIONAL VERSION® (NIV®). Copyright © 1973, 1978, 1984 by International Bible Society. Used by permission of Zondervan Publishing House. All rights reserved; the *New Revised Standard Version* (NRSV), copyright © 1989, by the Division of Christian Education of the National Council of the Churches of Christ in the USA, used by permission, all rights reserved; the *New King James Version* (NKJV). Copyright © 1982 by Thomas Nelson, Inc. Used by permission. All rights reserved; and the *King James Version* (KJV).

Willard, Dallas, 1935-
  Revolution of character : discovering Christ's pattern for spiritual
transformation / Dallas Willard with Don Simpson.
    p. cm.
  Includes bibliographical references.
  ISBN 1-57683-857-9
  1. Spiritual formation. I. Simpson, Don (Donald Howard), 1943- II.
Title.
  BV4511.W532 2005
  248.4--dc22

                    2005016745

Printed in Canada

2 3 4 5 6 7 / 10 09 08 07 06

FOR A FREE CATALOG OF
NAVPRESS BOOKS & BIBLE STUDIES,
CALL 1-800-366-7788 (USA) OR 1-800-839-4769 (CANADA)

Contents

Note to the Reader

This book is a distillation of *Renovation of the Heart* and is designed to make that book's contents more accessible and more useful for specific purposes. This book can simply be read and enjoyed as you would read a regular book. Or you can add to your reading a time of interaction with God in a setting where you normally have personal devotions. At the end of each chapter are suggestions for your meditation and response.

In addition, this book can become a guide for a retreat away from home in which you interact with God in an extended and more intense way. If you haven't done this before, the idea may seem strange or difficult. But this experience can be easier and more rewarding than you may think. It simply involves sitting quietly and expectantly for a day or more at a retreat center or hotel room of your choice, reading and listening for God's leading. Again, the questions at the end of each chapter can help prompt your meditation. You may wish to use just the first chapter or two during your retreat and then carry on your reading at other times during your normal weekly schedule.

You may want to keep a journal to record your thoughts related to the questions at the end of each chapter—as well as any other thoughts God may be stirring in you as you read through the book.

The aim of the book is spiritual change—a revolution of character. We suggest that you approach this crucial inner work in a way that fits your particular lifestyle.

The text of this book has been composed entirely by Don Simpson and expresses our shared understanding of *Renovation of the Heart*.

Dallas Willard

A Revolution Has Begun

*"Those who drink the water I give them will never
again be thirsty. The water I give will become in
them a spring of water gushing up to eternal life."*

JESUS OF NAZARETH, JOHN 4:14, PAR

We are created for a divine life.

When we open the writings of the New Testament, we discover
that we are called to live in the awareness of another world, to join
in "the kingdom of the heavens" and to "participate in the divine
nature."

The amazing promises given to those who devote themselves to
this new world leap out at us from the page. We read Jesus' words
that those who give their lives to him will receive "living water,"
the Spirit of God himself. This water will keep them from ever
being thirsty again—from being driven and ruled by unsatisfied
desires. This water will become a fountain "gushing up to eternal
life" (John 4:14, PAR). Indeed, it will even become "rivers of living
water" flowing from the center of the believer's life to a thirsty
world (John 7:38, NRSV).

Or we read the apostle Paul's prayer that believers will "know
the love of Christ that surpasses knowledge, so that they may be

filled with all the fullness of God . . . by the power at work within us, that is able to accomplish abundantly far more than all we can ask or imagine" (Ephesians 3:19-20, PAR).

Or we find the apostle Peter's words that those who love Jesus "rejoice with an indescribable and glorious joy" (1 Peter 1:8, NRSV) and "genuine mutual love" pouring from their hearts (1:22, NRSV), which rids them of "all malice, and all guile, insincerity, envy, and all slander" (2:1, NRSV).

What an astonishing vision! The water of heaven flows through our being until we are fully changed people. We wake each morning breathing the air of this new world; we experience a new consciousness, and our character is transformed. We drop our deceitful practices, our insincerity, our defensiveness, our envy, and our slander, and we move outward toward others in genuine love.

THE REALITY SHOW

But while this life is intensely attractive and desirable, we must admit the reality that Christians find their way into this divine life slowly and with great difficulty—if at all.

I believe one reason so many people fail to immerse themselves in the life described in the New Testament is that it is so unlike their own experience. This is true even though they may be quite faithful to their church and really do have Jesus Christ as their only hope. But the New Testament presentation of the life they are offered in Christ only discourages them. Instead of inspiring them, it makes them feel hopeless.

Why is this? Surely the life God holds out to us in Jesus was not meant to be an unsolvable puzzle! I suggest that for all our good intentions and strenuous efforts, *we don't approach and receive the life Jesus offers us in the right way.* We do not grasp the wisdom of Jesus concerning human life and his work of redemption in all its crucial dimensions.

It isn't always true that where there is a will, there is a way. When it comes to transforming human nature, we also need an understanding of the depth of our problem and how Christ works to redeem each element of our nature.

Jesus invites us to leave our burdensome ways of heavy labor—especially our "religious" ones—and step into the yoke of training with him. His is a way of gentleness and lowliness, a way of soul rest. His is a way of inner transformation in which carrying our burden *with him* is easy and light (see Matthew 11:28-30). What we thought was so difficult about entering fully into the divine life *is entirely due to our failure to understand and take the small steps that quietly but surely lead to our transformation.*

This is a hopeful, life-saving insight. It means that all the hindrances to our putting off the old person and putting on the new one *can be removed or mastered.* This "soul competence" will enable us to walk increasingly in the wholeness, holiness, and power of the kingdom of the heavens. No one needs to live in spiritual and personal defeat. A life of victory over sin and circumstance is accessible to us all.

WE LIVE FROM OUR HEART

Our life and how we respond to the world is a result of who we have become in the depths of our being. We call this inner being our spirit, our will—or, as a comprehensive term, our *heart*. From the contents of our heart, we see our world and interpret reality. From that decisive place in our self, we make choices, break forth into action, and try to change our world. We live from our depths—most of which we understand only in part.

However, the human self is not mysterious. There is an order to it that can be explored. We can influence its spiritual formation in a way that changes our entire outlook. In this book, we will seek a greater understanding of the elements and forces at work in our heart, and we will explore ways to shape our inner being "after God's own heart" (1 Samuel 13:14, PAR). Because a carefully cultivated heart—assisted by the grace of God—is able to transform even the most painful situations, we are able to handle with greater insight, gratitude, and redeeming grace situations that before would have caused us to stand like helpless children asking, "Why?"

Perhaps most satisfying, we will be able to connect with God at a deeper, more personal level of loving awareness and interaction. But further, a better understanding of our heart will enable us to influence situations in our families, businesses, and communities with greater godliness, effectiveness, and clarity. For the work of Christ always begins in our heart and moves outward into our everyday experiences.

To get to that place of increased self-knowledge, honesty,

humility before God, and a consistently Christlike attitude, we must step away in moments of reflection or even times of personal retreat to examine the inner workings of our human nature. Therefore, at the end of each chapter of this book, we will consider questions for thought or action that can be done either individually or in a group to aid us in this self-knowledge and transformation. The intent is flexibility, so use this book in a way that best suits you—whether in a retreat format or simply in daily time alone with God.

THE REVOLUTION OF JESUS

We must start with the inescapable relevance of Jesus. Jesus is the spiritual master who knows exactly *what* needs changing in our heart and *how* that change must come about. About two thousand years ago, he gathered his small group of friends and trainees on the Galilean hillsides and sent them out to "teach all nations." He sparked a movement to draw apprentices to himself from all ethnic groups. His continuing objective is to eventually bring all of human life under the direction of his wisdom, goodness, and power.

In sending out his disciples, Jesus set in motion a *perpetual world revolution*, one that is still in process and will continue until God's will is done on earth as it is in heaven. As this revolution culminates, all the forces of evil known to humankind will be defeated, and the goodness of God will be known, accepted, and joyously conformed to in every aspect of human life.[1]

The revolution of Jesus is first and always a revolution of

the human heart. His revolution does not proceed through the means of social institutions and laws—the outer forms of our existence—intending that these would then impose a good order of life upon people who come under their power. Rather, his is a *revolution of character*, which proceeds by changing people from the inside through ongoing personal relationship with God and one another. It is a revolution that changes people's ideas, beliefs, feelings, and habits of choice, as well as their bodily tendencies and social relations. It penetrates to the deepest layers of their soul. External, social arrangements may be useful to this end, but they are not the end, nor are they a fundamental part of the means.

On the other hand, from those divinely renovated depths of the person, social structures will naturally be transformed so that "justice roll[s] down like waters, and righteousness like an ever-flowing stream" (Amos 5:24, NRSV). Such streams *cannot* flow through corrupted souls. At the same time, a changed "within" will not cooperate with public streams of unrighteousness. A transformed soul will block those streams—or die trying.

The impotence of political and social systems to bring about real change is one reason Jesus didn't send his students out to start governments or even churches as we know them today. These organizations inevitably convey some elements of a human system. Instead, his disciples were to establish beachheads of his Person, word, and power in the midst of a failing and futile humanity. They were to bring the presence of the kingdom and its King into every corner of human life by fully living in the kingdom with him.

Those who received him as their living Lord and instructor would be "God's chosen ones, holy and beloved" (Colossians 3:12, NRSV). They would learn how to "be blameless and harmless, children of God, faultless in the midst of a twisted and misguided generation, from within which they shine as lights in the world, lifting up a word of life" (Philippians 2:15-16, PAR).

Churches—thinking now of local assemblies of Christ's followers—would naturally result from this new kind of life. Churches are not the kingdom of God, but they are primary expressions, outposts, and instruments of the presence of the kingdom among us. They are "societies" of Jesus, springing up in Jerusalem, Judea, Samaria, and to the furthest points on earth (see Acts 1:8) as the reality of Christ is brought to bear on ordinary human life. This is an ongoing process, not yet completed today: "This gospel of the kingdom shall be preached in the whole world as a testimony to all the nations, and then the end will come" (Matthew 24:14).

OUR HIDDEN LIFE

On the conscious surface of our "world within" lie some of our thoughts, feelings, intentions, and plans. These are the ones we are aware of. They may be fairly obvious to others as well as to ourselves.

But what we really think, how we really feel, and what we really would do in circumstances unforeseen are often totally unknown to us and to those who know us. We may pass one another—even pass ourselves, if we can imagine that—like "ships in the night."

In other words, the hidden dimension of our life is not visible to others, nor are we fully able to grasp it ourselves. We usually know very little about the things that move in our own soul, the deepest level of our life. Our "within" is astonishingly complex and subtle—even devious. It takes on a life of its own. Only God knows our depths, who we are, and what we would do in any given situation.

The psalmist cried out for God's help in dealing with—himself! "Search me, O God" (139:23, NRSV). "Let the meditations of my heart be acceptable to you" (19:14, PAR). "Renew in me a right spirit" (51:10, PAR). At a certain point in life, our "within" (our heart) has been formed, and we are then at its mercy. Only God can save us.

SPIRITUAL FORMATION

Although every human being is formed spiritually—for better or for worse—spiritual formation for the Christian refers to the *Holy Spirit–driven process* of forming the inner world of the human self in such a way that it becomes like the inner being of Christ himself.[2] To the degree spiritual formation in Christ is successful, the outer life of the individual becomes a natural expression of the character and teachings of Jesus.

Christian spiritual formation is focused entirely on Jesus. Its goal is conformity to Christ, a process that arises out of purposeful interaction with the grace of God in Christ. Obedience is an essential outcome (see John 13:34-35; 14:21).

However, we cannot manifest Christlikeness through a primary focus on external behavior. When externals are the main emphasis, spiritual formation doesn't really happen. The process falls into deadening legalisms. This is what has happened so often in the past. Peculiar modes of dress, behavior, and organization don't change the heart.

Externalism was a danger even in New Testament times. But "that Christ be formed within you" has always been the true watchword of Christian spiritual formation (Galatians 4:19, PAR). This watchword is fortified by the deep moral and spiritual insight that while "the letter of the law kills, the spirit gives life" (2 Corinthians 3:6, PAR).

To illustrate briefly, Jesus' teachings in the Sermon on the Mount (see Matthew 5–7) refer to various wrong behaviors: acting out in anger, looking so as to lust, heartless divorce, verbal manipulation, returning evil for evil, and so forth.[3] But as abundant experience teaches, to strive merely to *act* in conformity with Jesus' expressions of what living in the kingdom of God is like is to attempt the impossible. We may work hard at it and keep up a good front for a while, but eventually we fall flat on our faces.

THE WAY OF GRACE

The influences in spiritual formation involve much more than human effort. Well-informed human effort is indispensable, of course, because spiritual formation is not a passive process. But Christlikeness of the inner being is not, finally, a human attainment. It is a gift of grace.

So we must draw on resources far beyond our own action. We must rely on the interactive presence of the Holy Spirit in our life.

And we must become familiar with the spiritual treasures stored in the body of Christ's people: the invaluable persons, events, traditions, and teachings of the past and present.

The Spirit uses the spiritual riches of Christ's continuing incarnation in his people, including the treasures of his written and spoken Word and the amazing personalities of those in whom he has most fully lived. Again, deep character change is a gift of grace, but we can seek this grace through humility and the ancient disciplines of spiritual formation. That is the path we will pursue in the course of this book.

Spiritual formation is the way of rest for the weary and overloaded, the easy yoke and the light burden (see Matthew 11:28-30), the cleaning of the inside of the cup and dish (see Matthew 23:26). It is the way of the good tree that cannot bear bad fruit (see Luke 6:43).

Jesus still calls his disciples "to do all things that I have commanded you" within the context of his authority and personal presence: "I have been given say over everything in heaven and earth" (Matthew 28:18, PAR) and "Look, I am with you every moment" (verse 20, PAR).

But, to reemphasize because it is so important, our aim is not first to act differently but to *become different in our inner being*. We're not just learning how to be nicer versions of our old selves. We're dealing radically with the fundamental wrongness of human life left to itself and introducing the kingdom of righteousness that is Christ into the depths of our heart. It is the inner life that counts. That is where profound transformation must occur.

The apostle Paul wrote that when we persevere in the

revolution of our character, placing our hope in Christ alone, we won't be disappointed because "God has poured out his love *into* our hearts by the Holy Spirit, whom he has given us" (Romans 5:5, NIV, emphasis added). It is the love of God flowing through us—not our human attempts at behavioral change—that becomes "a spring of water gushing up to eternal life" (John 4:14, PAR). This love has the power to "always protect, always trust, always hope, put up with anything, and never quit" (1 Corinthians 13:7-8, PAR). This love will become a constant source of joy and refreshment to ourselves and to others.

Transformation is possible because our inner being is an orderly realm where, even in the disorder of its brokenness, God has provided a methodical path of recovery. Grace does not rule out method, nor method grace. Grace thrives on method and method on grace.

So spiritual formation is both a profound manifestation of God's gracious action through his Word and Spirit *and* something we are responsible for before God and can set about achieving in a sensible, systematic manner.

The aim of this book is intensely practical. It is a guide for all who deeply desire to attain the inner life of Jesus Christ himself, allowing him to

> Be of sin the double cure,
> Save from wrath and make me pure.[4]

Questions for Meditation and Response

1. The revolution of character begins with vision—a vision of what things will be like if and when the revolution takes place. After reading chapter 1, how would you describe the person you can become—inwardly and outwardly—if you pursue this revolution?

2. How might a revolution in you affect your family, coworkers, and others around you?

3. When you think about becoming that sort of person, what positive thoughts and feelings arise in your mind? Negative thoughts and feelings? (Try to notice and write them down without editing them.)

4. Describe a situation in which you were surprised or dismayed at something you found yourself saying or doing. If you can't think of one, ask God to show you. (This could be something you try to notice over the coming week and note in your journal.)

5. In the past, how have you tried to deal with besetting sins or careless words that seem to pop out of your mouth automatically?

6. Pray that as you read further in this book, God will build in you a vision of what he can accomplish in you if you cooperate

with his Holy Spirit in transforming your heart. (You might want to write this prayer down.)

7. Meditate on Matthew 11:28-30. What do Jesus' words here mean? Do you have questions about any parts of this passage? What thoughts and feelings arise in you in response to Jesus' words?

Chapter 2

The Heart,
Center of Our Life

*A certain expert stood up to check Jesus out, saying,
"Teacher, what shall I do to receive eternal life?"*

*Jesus responded, "What does the law say? How
do you read it?"*

*And he answered, "You shall love the Lord
your God with all your heart, and with all your
soul, and with all your strength, and with all your
mind; and your neighbor as yourself."*

*And Jesus said, "Well, there you have your
answer. Do that and you will live."*

LUKE 10:25-28, PAR

TAKING CARE OF OUR CORE

If we aim to form our heart in godliness, we must understand
what our heart is and how it works in the overall system of personal
life. When I speak of our heart, I refer to that center or inner core
of our being from which all our actions flow.

Those with well-kept hearts are persons who are prepared to
respond to the situations of life in ways that are good and right.

They choose what is good and avoid what is evil, and as they "grow in grace," all the components of their nature increasingly cooperate with these choices. This kind of person is not perfect, of course, but what all people manage in life sometimes, the person with the well-kept heart manages as a general rule.

But before we reach the ideal of a well-kept heart, we are often divided into incoherent fragments. We are like the man described in Proverbs:

> *Like a city that is broken into and without walls*
> *Is a man who has no control over his spirit.*
> *(Proverbs 25:28)*

The ideal calls us forward because "a house divided cannot stand" (Luke 11:17, PAR). Only to the degree that we come close to the ideal are our lives well directed or even coherent. In a world deeply infected by evil, few people do what their own heart tells them is good and right—and all too often this is also true with whole groups of people.

How rare it is to find a group that consistently functions well toward the good it envisions! In fact, a group usually exhibits the divided hearts and lives of its members even more strikingly than does the individual alone. This is because of its larger scope and greater complexity. When successful, spiritual transformation unites the divided heart of the individual. That person can then bring remarkable harmony into the groups in which he or she participates.

THE SIX BASIC ELEMENTS OF A PERSON

Although our heart is our center (it's the part of our person that reflects our character), spiritual transformation happens best when we work on the elements of our self in a specific order. When we take a closer look at the whole person, we find that there are six basic aspects in our lives as individual human beings—six things inseparable from every human life. Placed in the best order for spiritual transformation, these are the elements of human nature:

1. Thoughts (images, concepts, judgments, inferences)

2. Feelings (sensations, emotions)

3. Heart, also called "spirit" and "will" (choice, decision; reflected as *character*)

4. Body (action; interacts with the physical world)

5. Social context (personal and structural relations with others)

6. Soul (the factor that integrates all of the above to form one life)

As we proceed in this book, I will show you how the first two elements—thoughts and feelings—really combine to form a single functioning part, which we will call the mind. But for now,

I want to speak of thoughts and feelings separately to highlight their uniqueness. Also, at first glance, you may find some of these six dimensions confusingly close to one another in meaning (for example, the heart and the soul). But please stay with me. In the chapters ahead, we will look carefully at each part in detail. For now, I hope to give you a brief overview to explain how these parts of the self operate together and why the spiritual health of each is so important.

The ideal of the spiritual life occurs when all six essential parts of the human self are effectively attuned to God as they are restored and sustained by him. *Spiritual formation in Christ is the* process *leading toward that ideal end—the self fully integrated and attuned to God. To mature in spiritual formation means to love God with* all *of the heart, soul, mind, and strength and to love one's neighbor as oneself.*

The salvation of the believer in Christ is essentially holistic or whole-life. David the psalmist, speaking of his own experience (but prophetically expressing the perspective of Jesus the Messiah), said,

> *I bless the Lord who gives me counsel;*
>> *in the night also my heart instructs me.*
> *I keep the Lord always before me;*
>> *because he is at my right hand, I shall not be moved.*
>
> *Therefore my heart is glad, and my soul rejoices;*
>> *my body also rests secure. (Psalm 16:7-9, NRSV)*

Note how many aspects of the self are explicitly involved in this passage: the thoughts, the feelings, the heart, the soul, the body, and the social or relational context (in this instance, God).

A QUICK LOOK AT THE
SIX HUMAN DIMENSIONS

Thoughts

Thoughts bring objects or ideas before our mind in various ways and enable us to ponder them and trace out their interrelationships with one another. Thoughts are what empower our heart to range far beyond the immediate boundaries of our environment and the limited perceptions of our senses. Through them, our consciousness is able to reach into the depths of the universe—past, present, and future—by reasoning and scientific thinking, by imagination and art, and also by divine revelation, which comes to us mainly in the form of thought.

Feelings

Feelings incline us toward or away from things that come before our mind in thought. Feelings involve a tone that is pleasant or painful, along with an attraction or repulsion concerning what's in our thoughts. How we feel about food, automobiles, relationships, positions in life, and hundreds of other things illustrates this point.

Notice that feelings and thoughts always go together. They are interdependent and are never found apart. There is no feeling without something being before our mind in thought and no thought without some positive or negative feeling toward what we contemplate. What we call indifference is never a total absence of feeling but simply an unusually low degree of feeling, usually negative.

Once again, the connection between thoughts and feelings is so intimate that the mind is usually treated as consisting of thoughts and feelings *together*. I will keep them together as "mind" in this book. Of course, the mind is a complicated aspect of the person, with numerous subdivisions built into both thoughts and feelings. In the sin-ruined soul, the mind becomes a fearful wilderness and a wild mixture of thoughts and feelings manifested in willful stupidities, blatant inconsistencies, and confusions—often to the point of obsession, madness, or possession. This condition of mind is what characterizes our world apart from God. Satan, "the prince of this world" (John 12:31; 14:30, NIV), holds sway over it.

Heart

Let's look further at important aspects of the heart. Volition, or will, is the particular exercise of the heart to *originate* things and events that would not otherwise occur. Involving both freedom and creativity, the power to originate is the *power to do what is good—or evil*.

Although a free action has many conditions, there is always the unforced yes or no by which a person responds to a situation. This response is our unique contribution to reality. It is *our* action—it is *we* who are responding to something.

Without the inner yes, there is no sin. The mere *thought* of sin is not sin and is not even temptation. Temptation is the thought plus the inclination to sin—possibly manifested by lingering over the thought or seeking it out. But sin itself is when we inwardly say yes to the temptation, when we *decide* to do the deed, even though we may not *actually* do it.

The heart's capacity for volition and the acts in which volition is exercised form what's known as the *spirit* in man. If we are to understand spiritual formation, we must understand what the spirit of the human being is. Only God is pure spirit—pure creative will and character. He is unbodily, personal power. Only he can truly say, "I AM THAT I AM" (Exodus 3:14, KJV).

But human beings have some small element of spirit—unbodily, personal power—right at the *center* of who they are and who they become. Above all, it is this spirit (or heart) that must be reached, cared for, and transformed in spiritual formation. The human spirit is primarily what must be given a godly nature and must then proceed to expand its godly governance over the entire personality.

Because the *spirit* is also the *heart* in the human system—the *core* of our being, we could say—we have the biblical teaching that human good and evil are matters of the heart. It is the heart and spirit that God looks at (see 1 Samuel 16:7; Isaiah 66:2) in relating to humankind and in allowing us to relate to him (see 2 Chronicles 15:4,15; Jeremiah 29:13; Hebrews 11:6).

Life must be organized by the heart if it is to be organized at all. It can be pulled together only from the inside. That is the function of the heart, spirit, or will: to organize our life as a whole, and, indeed, to organize it around God. A great part of the disaster of contemporary life lies in the fact that it is organized around our human feelings, not around God.

Body

The body is our personal presence in the physical and social world. In union with it, we come into existence and become the persons we shall forever be. The body is our primary energy source or strength—our personalized "power pack"—a place where we can even stand in defiance of God, at least for a while. And it is the point through which we are stimulated by the world beyond ourselves and through which we touch and are touched by others.[1]

Personal relationships cannot be separated from the body. On the other hand, the body cannot be understood apart from human relations. It is essentially social. Therefore, our bodies are forever a part of our identities as persons.

We live *from* our bodies. Our choices, as they settle into character (which we will explore more later), are "outsourced" to our body in its social context. Most of our choices occur more or less automatically without our having to think about what we are doing. And that is generally a very good thing. Just recall how cumbersome it is when we *have* to think about what we are doing—learning to skate, drive a car, speak a language. The very purpose of learning or training in some activity is to bring it under our direction so we will no longer have to think about it. The body makes this possible. It has a tacit "knowledge" of its own.

Of course, this basically good and even glorious feature of the body—its capacity to "have a life of its own," as we might say—is also a major problem for spiritual formation. Trained in a world of wrongness and evil, the body comes to act wrongly before we can think. It has motions of sin in its members, as the apostle Paul said (see Romans 7:23), which may thwart the true intent of our heart by leaping ahead of it.

"It is not me," Paul cried, "but sin that dwells in me!" (Romans 7:17, PAR). He went on to say, "The flesh wants what is contrary to the spirit and the spirit what is contrary to the flesh. They are in opposition to each other, so that it is impossible for you to do what you really want" (Galatians 5:17, PAR).

But at the same time, this amazing capacity of the body means that it (like the other dimensions of human life) can be re-formed to become our ally in Christlikeness. Such a re-formation of the body is one major part of the process of spiritual formation, as we shall see. The body is not, in the biblical view, essentially evil; and, while it is infected with evil, it can be delivered. Spiritual formation is in many ways a bodily process. It cannot succeed unless the body is also transformed.

Social Context

The human self requires rootedness in others. The most fundamental "other" for the human is, of course, God himself. God is the ultimate social fact for the human being. That is why people in general think more often about God than about any other thing, even sex and death. But because we are *all* rooted in God—whether we want to be or not—our ties to one another cannot be isolated from our shared relationship to God. Nor can our relationship to him be cut off from our ties to one another.

"If someone says, 'I love God,' and hates his brother, he is a liar," John wrote unapologetically, "for the one who does not love his brother whom he has seen, cannot love God whom he has not seen" (1 John 4:20). We live as we should only when we are in a right relation to God and to other human beings—therefore, we have the two Great Commandments.

It's been shown that an infant who is not received in love by its mother and others is wounded for life and may even die. It must bond with its mother or with *someone* in order to take on a self. Rejection, no matter how old one is, is a sword thrust through the soul that has literally killed many. Largely unbeknownst to itself, Western society is a culture of rejection. This is one of the irreversible effects of modernity, a collection of impersonal powers that deeply affects the social institutions (even Christian institutions) of our time. It seeps into our soul as a deadly enemy to spiritual formation in Christ.

Our relations with others have incalculable importance for the formation of our spirit, for better or for worse. And our body is the conduit of these relations—from its physical composition and "looks" (how we appear to others and how we observe them) to the way we touch, work, talk, and pray together.

But our social dimension is also inseparable from our *inner* thoughts, feelings, and choices. Their existence is influenced by our social setting. Our very relation to Christ our Savior, teacher, and friend is located in the social dimension. This is true as well of our place in Christ's body on earth—his continuing incarnation, the church.

Soul

The soul is that dimension of the person that connects all of the other dimensions so that they form one life. It is a higher-level dimension because its direct field of play consists of the other dimensions (thoughts, body, and so on). It reaches deep into the person's vast environment of God and his creation. It has been said that each soul is a star in the spiritual universe—or so it was meant to be (see Matthew 13:43). This is the biblical view, understanding that "soul" refers to the whole person through its most profound dimension.

Because the soul encompasses the whole person, it is frequently taken to *be* the person. We naturally treat persons as souls. But the soul is not the person. It is, rather, the deepest part of the self in terms of overall operations. Like the body, it operates without conscious supervision.

The soul is somewhat like a computer that quietly runs a business or manufacturing operation and comes to our attention only when it malfunctions or requires adaptation to new tasks. It can be significantly "reprogrammed," and this is a major part of what goes into the spiritual formation (re-formation) of the person.

Because the soul is to some degree independent of conscious direction, biblical language often addresses it in the third person. The psalmist asked,

> *Why are you in despair, O my soul?*
> *And why have you become disturbed within me?*
> *Hope in God, for I shall again praise Him*
> *For the help of His presence." (42:5)*

The rich fool of Luke 12 said, "I will say to my soul, 'Soul, you have many goods laid up for many years to come; take your ease, eat, drink, and be merry'" (verse 19).

But for all of the soul's independence, the tiny executive center of the person—that is, the heart (spirit or will)—can redirect and re-form the soul with God's participation. It mainly does this by redirecting the body in spiritual disciplines and toward various other types of experiences under God.

THE WHOLE PICTURE

Now, with all of this said, it will be useful for our purposes to depict the entire human self with the following diagram:

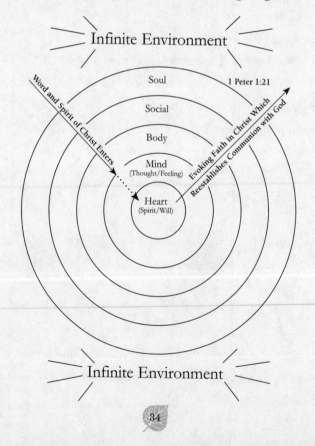

Diagrams of nonphysical realities are always inadequate depictions, but they can still be helpful. Notice: (a) the mind includes thoughts and feelings, and (b) the inner circles are not meant to *exclude* the outer ones but to incorporate them in part. For example, there is more to the mind than there is to the heart, though the heart interacts with the mind; there is more to the body than there is to the mind, though the mind interacts with the body; and so on. As the outer circle, the soul interfaces with an infinite environment. As the most inclusive dimension of the self, the soul is foundational to all others.

It is possible for forces entirely outside the person to achieve access to the soul. This access can come from God, certainly, but possibly from other forces as well, benign or dreadful. The soul can be sustained and function properly only in the safekeeping of God. "Behold, all souls are Mine," says the Lord (Ezekiel 18:4).

The arrows in the diagram show the movement of grace in the life of the person who is being spiritually formed. As we proceed in chapters to come, we will examine how the Word and Spirit enter the heart of a person and how faith in Christ and communion with God come forth.

INFLUENCE ON ACTION

But now we turn to action in the life of a person. Our actions *always* arise out of the *interplay* of the elements in human life: heart, thoughts, feelings, body, social relations, and soul. Action never comes from the movement of the will (heart) alone, for example. Understanding this is necessary for the practice of spiritual formation, which is bound to fail if it focuses on the will alone.

The inadequacy of good intentions by themselves to ensure proper action is marked by Jesus' words: "The spirit is willing, but the flesh is weak" (Matthew 26:41). If the six dimensions are properly aligned with God and with what is good, our actions will simply be the good fruit of a good tree. If they are not so aligned, they will be the inevitable bad fruit of a bad tree.

A wrong alignment is characteristic of what Paul described as "the mind set on the flesh," which is "death." However, "the mind set on the Spirit is life and peace" (Romans 8:6). For the individual away from God, "flesh" becomes simply the body. When the body is our main concern, it is impossible to please God, and our life is utter futility, as Paul explained to the Romans:

> *For those who live according to the flesh set their minds on the things of the flesh, but those who live according to the Spirit set their minds on the things of the Spirit. To set the mind on the flesh is death, but to set the mind on the Spirit is life and peace. For this reason the mind that is set on the flesh is hostile to God; it does not submit to God's law—indeed it cannot, and those who are in the flesh cannot please God. (8:5-8, NRSV)*

When the proper ordering of the human system under God is complete—which will never *fully* occur in this life because of the complexity of our nature and the conflicted spiritual environment that surrounds us—then we become people who "love God with all their heart, and with all their soul, and with all their strength and with all their mind; and their neighbor as themselves" (Luke 10:27, PAR; see also Mark 12:30-33). When we are like this, our whole life is an eternal one. Everything we do counts for eternity and is preserved there (see Colossians 3:17).

Once our spirit comes alive in God, the lengthy process of subduing all aspects of the self under God can begin. This is the process of spiritual formation viewed in its entirety. *Spiritual transformation happens only as each essential dimension of the human being is transformed to Christlikeness under the direction of a regenerate will interacting with constant overtures of grace from God. Such transformation is not the result of mere human effort and cannot be accomplished by putting pressure on the will (heart, spirit) alone.*

Questions for Meditation and Response

1. Describe what your heart is and does. Give a personal example of your heart in action.

2. Give an example of each of these from your life recently:
   • a thought
   • a feeling connected to that thought

3. On pages 28–29 a distinction is drawn between a thought, a temptation, and a sin. Here is an example:

   Thought: "I could say something cutting about Person X to Person Y."

Temptation: "I suppose I could. Person Y would be quite amused. What could I say?"

Sin: "I could say she waddles like a duck. I will say it—ah, but now Person Z has arrived and is talking a mile a minute. Maybe later."

Now it's your turn. Make up one or more examples of a thought, temptation, and sin so that the progression is clear in your mind.

4. Spirit is "unbodily, personal power." How is that like and unlike each of these kinds of power: electricity, water turning the wheel of a mill, horses pulling a cart, a human arm turning a crank?

5. Describe a recent time when you wanted to do something good, but your automatic bodily habit, feeling, or thought wouldn't go along.

6. Reflect prayerfully on Romans 8:5-7. For instance, what does it mean to "live according to the flesh"? What does it mean to "set the mind on the flesh"? Think of an example of something fleshly that a person could focus his mind on. Ask God to help you set your mind on the Spirit and grasp the value of doing so.

A Magnificent Ruin

The Lord looks down from heaven on humankind
to see if there are any who are wise, who seek after
God. They have all gone astray, they are all alike
perverse; there is no one who does good, no, not
one.

PSALM 14:2-3, PAR

THE RADICAL RUIN OF OUR SOUL

Before we can grasp the need for a revolution of character, we must see the human soul in its state of profound ruin. Remember that all people undergo a process of spiritual formation. No one escapes. From the most hardened criminal to the most devout person, everyone has had *some form of spiritual formation.* In one of C. S. Lewis's more striking passages, he challenges us to remember this:

> *The dullest and most uninteresting person you*
> *talk to may one day be a creature which, if you saw*
> *it now, you would be strongly tempted to worship,*
> *or else a horror and a corruption such as you now*
> *meet, if at all, only in a nightmare. . . . There are*

no ordinary people. You have never talked to a mere mortal. Nations, cultures, arts, civilizations— these are mortal, and their life is to ours as the life of a gnat. But it is immortals whom we joke with, work with, marry, snub, and exploit—immortal horrors or everlasting splendors.[1]

Strangely, it is precisely the intrinsic greatness of the person that makes it "a horror and a corruption such as you now meet . . . only in a nightmare." If we were insignificant, our ruin would not be horrifying. G. K. Chesterton says that the hardest thing to accept in the Christian religion is the great value it places upon the individual soul. Still older Christian writers used to say that God hid the majesty of the human soul from us to prevent our being ruined by vanity.

This explains why even in its ruined condition, a human being is regarded by God as something infinitely worth saving. Sin does not make a person worthless—only lost. And in its lostness, the human soul is still capable of great strength, creativity, dignity, and heartbreaking beauty.

"Sin" Has Left Our Language

In our present thought world, the horror of our ruin is hidden from polite and enlightened conversation. Sin as a condition of the human self is not available philosophically or ethically to explain why life proceeds the way it does. For example, why do around half of American marriages fail, or why do we have massive problems with substance addiction and with the "moral failures" of public leaders? The thinkers who are supposed to know such things are lost in speculation about "causes." Meanwhile, the real source of our failures lies in our *choices* and the factors at work in them. *Choice is where the potential for sin dwells.*

Our social and psychological sciences stand helpless before the terrible things done by human beings. But the warped nature of the human will—the reality of sin—is something we are not allowed to admit into "serious" discussion. We are like farmers who diligently plant crops but can't admit the existence of weeds and insects and can only think to pour on more fertilizer. Similarly, the only solution we know to human problems today is "education."

But education as now understood *cannot* come to grips with the reality of the human self. It is not just a matter of "separation of church and state." Rather, most educational institutions today have adopted values, attitudes, and practices that make any rigorous understanding of the human self and its life impossible.

Soul Ruin in the Church

A few years ago, within a period of a few weeks, three nationally known pastors in Southern California were publicly exposed for sexual sins. But sex is far from being our only problem in the church. The presence of vanity, egotism, hostility, fear, indifference, and downright meanness can be counted among professing Christians. The opposites of those qualities—the fruit of the Spirit—cannot be simply assumed in the typical Christian group. The rare individual who exemplifies genuine purity and humility, death to selfishness, freedom from anger and rage, and so on will stand out in the group with all the obtrusiveness of a sore thumb. He or she will be a constant hindrance in group processes and will be personally conflicted by those processes, for that person will not be living on the same terms as the others.

AND BEYOND THE CHURCH

The church is answerable for its condition, but so is the rest of humanity. The apostle Peter wrote, "If judgment first begins at the house of God, what shall be the outcome for those who give no heed to the gospel of God? And if it is difficult for the righteous to be saved, what will happen to the godless and rebellious?" (1 Peter 4:17, PAR).

The fact is, the situation outside the church is much worse than within. The news, courts, law offices, community, families, and educational and penal institutions provide a constant outpouring of wrongdoing that wells up from the malformed human spirit, mind, soul, body, and social relations.

Diogenes, the ancient Greek, lit a lantern and walked the streets of Athens at noonday looking for an honest man. He never found one, it is said. But in the church, as in life generally, few are ready to deal with the realities of the deeper self—in themselves or in others.

THE PROPHETIC WITNESS

The Bible's prophetic illumination of the human soul in its lostness is starkly clear and repeated over and over, from Moses and Samuel to Jesus, Paul, and John. When the prophet Jeremiah says,

> *"The heart is more deceitful than all else*
> *And is desperately sick;*
> *Who can understand it?" (17:9),*

we have to recognize from our heart that *we* are the ones spoken of. Only with this confession is a foundation laid for formation into Christlikeness.

Our initial move toward Christlikeness cannot be toward self-esteem. Realistically, I'm *not* okay, and you're *not* okay. We're all in serious trouble. That must be our starting point. Self-esteem in our situation will only breed self-deception and frustration. Regardless of what we may say to "pump ourselves up" or what others might tell us, we are better off not concealing or denying who we really are.

Jesus addressed leaders of his day in language that may seem harsh to us, but that was the only way he could be of help to them. As strong as their self-defenses were, they needed strong medicine. He chastised them, saying, "You Pharisees clean the outside of the dish, but your insides are full of greed and filth. How foolish of you! Isn't God as interested in your insides as your outside?" (Luke 11:39-40, PAR), and, "If you wash a dish well on the inside, won't the outside come clean in the process?" (Matthew 23:26, PAR).

PAUL'S SUMMARY

Of course, the Pharisees had greater responsibility than ordinary people, but they were not necessarily more sinful. The condition Jesus addressed in them is the *human* condition. The Pharisee only made the true human condition more obvious by his pronouncements of righteousness and flamboyant religiosity. A former Pharisee himself, the apostle Paul summarized the prophetic account of the human self and traced the problem to its root:

> "THERE IS NONE RIGHTEOUS, NOT EVEN ONE;
>
> THERE IS NONE WHO UNDERSTANDS,
>
> THERE IS NONE WHO SEEKS FOR GOD;
>
> ALL HAVE TURNED ASIDE, TOGETHER THEY HAVE BECOME
>
> USELESS;
>
> THERE IS NONE WHO DOES GOOD,
>
> THERE IS NOT EVEN ONE."
>
> "THEIR THROAT IS AN OPEN GRAVE,
>
> WITH THEIR TONGUES THEY KEEP DECEIVING."
>
> "THE POISON OF ASPS IS UNDER THEIR LIPS";
>
> "WHOSE MOUTH IS FULL OF CURSING AND BITTERNESS";
>
> "THEIR FEET ARE SWIFT TO SHED BLOOD,
>
> DESTRUCTION AND MISERY ARE IN THEIR PATHS,
>
> AND THE PATH OF PEACE HAVE THEY NOT KNOWN."
>
> "THERE IS NO FEAR OF GOD BEFORE THEIR EYES."

(ROMANS 3:10-18)

44

The very last statement from this collection of Old Testament diagnoses of the human condition reaches to the core of the matter: "THERE IS NO FEAR OF GOD BEFORE THEIR EYES." Fear of God, the proverb tells us, is the beginning of wisdom (see Proverbs 9:10). Although not the outcome of wisdom, to be sure, it *is* the indispensable beginning. One *begins* to get smart when he or she fears being crosswise of God—fears not doing what he wants and not being as he requires.

Fear is the anticipation of harm. God is not mean, but he is dangerous, just as are some of the great forces he has placed in reality. Electricity and nuclear power, for example, are not mean, but they are dangerous. In a certain sense, if we don't "worry" about God, we simply aren't being smart. And that is the point of the verse.

TRUE UNDERSTANDING

"Knowledge of the Holy One is understanding," Proverbs 9:10 concludes (NIV). "Knowledge" in biblical language never refers to what we call "head knowledge" today but always to *experiential involvement* with what is known—to actual engagement with it. Jesus defines the quality of eternal life that he gives his people in this way: "that they might know thee the only true God, and Jesus Christ, whom thou hast sent" (John 17:3, KJV). He is speaking of the grace of constant, close interaction with the Trinitarian being of God. That is the life Jesus brings into the lives of those who seek and find him.

This is a deeper and fuller understanding of Proverbs 3:5-8:

> *Trust in the Lord with all your heart,*
> > *and do not rely exclusively on your own*
> > > *understanding.*
> *In all your ways acknowledge him,*
> > *and he will smooth your paths.*
> *Don't imagine you've got it all figured out.*
> > *Be afraid of the Lord and avoid evil.*
> *It will heal your body*
> > *and bring refreshment to your bones.* (PAR)

NOT-GOD

Trust in God is precisely what is absent from the ruined heart. In Romans 1, Paul described the progressive departure from God that spirals down into the perversions we see all around us—and within ourselves as well, if we are not being thoroughly transformed by Christ. As we might expect from the passages we've looked at, the slide into pervasive soul corruption begins with the heart (and its willfulness), deflecting the mind from God.

Human beings have always known there is a God, and they have understood to some degree what he is like (see Romans 1:19-20). But they were not pleased that God should have the most exalted place in the universe merely because he is who he is. And this is the key to understanding humanity's present condition. The first of the Ten Commandments deals with this inclination away from God (see Exodus 20:2-3). As Saint Augustine clearly saw, God being God offends human pride. If God is running the universe and has first claim on our lives, guess who *isn't* running the universe and does *not* get to have things as they please?

Philip Yancey tells us,

> *The historian of Alcoholics Anonymous titled his work Not-God because, he said, that stands as the most important hurdle an addicted person must surmount: to acknowledge, deep in the soul, not being God. No mastery of manipulation and control, at which alcoholics excel, can overcome the root problem; rather, the alcoholic must recognize individual helplessness and fall back in the arms of the Higher Power. "First of all, we had to quit playing God," concluded the founders of AA; and then allow God himself to "play God" in the addict's life, which involves daily, even moment-by-moment, surrender.*[2]

Denial and Its Effects

When we assume the place of God in our life, the power of *denial* comes into play. Denial of reality accounts for our perpetual blindness to the obvious. Human affairs at every level are affected by it. Denial alone explains why "the rulers of this age" do the things they do—up to the crucifixion of "the Lord of glory" himself (1 Corinthians 2:8, NRSV).

Denial of reality is inseparable from our fallen human heart, and its great power comes from not being recognized for what it is. The fact is, in a world apart from God, the power of denial is absolutely essential if life is to proceed. The human heart cannot—psychologically *cannot*—sustain itself for any length of time in the face of reality. We can't ponder our own death, we can't examine the conflicted nature of our motives and actions, we can't face our fears about other people—nor can we live with our own past or face our future—without profound denial. When we eliminate the light of God from our heart, our mind becomes dysfunctional, trying to devise a "truth" that will be compatible with the basic falsehood that man is god. Then, our feelings (emotions, affections, sensations) soon follow along the path to chaos. "They became futile in their speculations," Paul wrote, "and their foolish heart was darkened. Professing to be wise, they became fools" (Romans 1:21-22).

Sensuality Becomes Central

For the person who does not live interactively with God, the human body becomes the primary area of focus—usually for pleasure. Human beings turn to worship "the creature rather than the Creator" (Romans 1:25, NRSV). And because bodily enjoyment is what they *choose* to pursue, God abandons them to their pursuit of every pleasurable sensation. This is primarily sexual sensation, for that usually gives the greatest "kick." But bodily violence is a close second. This is the spiritual root of obsession with "sex and violence" in decadent societies.

But then it turns out that sensuality *cannot* be satisfied.

Ironically, sensuality deadens feeling. This awakens the relentless drive, the desperate need, simply *to feel*, to feel *something*. This drive is rooted in basic human nature, as we shall soon see. We have to have feeling, and it needs to be deep and sustained. But if we are not living the great drama of goodness in God's kingdom, the body's sensuality is all that is left in our "kingdom."

Paul made this observation to the Ephesians:

> *The Gentiles [those not knowing God] also walk, in the futility of their mind, being darkened in their understanding, excluded from the life of God because of the ignorance that is in them, because of the hardness of their heart; and they, having become callous, have given themselves over to sensuality for the practice of every kind of impurity with greediness. (4:17-19)*

This is the natural progression in the flight from God. The human drive to self-gratification opens up a life without boundaries, where nothing is forbidden—if one can get away with it. "Why?" is replaced with "Why not?" And because this is what these "gods" want—total license—God abandons them to a worthless mind: "As they did not see fit to center their knowledge upon God, God released them into the grip of a nonfunctional mind, to do what is indecent" (Romans 1:28, PAR).

The terrible outcome is a humanity "filled with all unrighteousness, wickedness, greed, evil; full of envy, murder, strife, deceit, malice; they are gossips, slanderers, haters of God, insolent, arrogant, boastful, inventors of evil, disobedient to parents, without understanding, untrustworthy, unloving, unmerciful." And although they know in reflective moments that God condemns such things, "they not only do the same, but also give hearty approval to those who practice them" (Romans 1:29-32).

Still True Today

The apostle Paul was not hopeful that things would get better as human history moved along. He was not a believer in "progress" as we speak of it today. He warned Timothy,

> *In the last days difficult times will come. For men will be lovers of self, lovers of money, boastful, arrogant, revilers, disobedient to parents, ungrateful, unholy, unloving, irreconcilable, malicious gossips, without self-control, brutal, haters of good, treacherous, reckless, conceited, lovers of pleasure rather than lovers of God, holding to a form of godliness, although they have denied its power. (2 Timothy 3:1-5)*

Who does not recognize in these words the prevailing tone of contemporary life? Who does not know that such behavior is excused and even justified by clever psychological, legal, and moral maneuvers, often reciting elevated "principles"?

But the Bible's prophetic clarity still stands for all to read. Our human righteousness is like "filthy rags" (Isaiah 64:6, KJV).

We hear,

> *"I, the LORD, search the heart,*
> *I test the mind,*
> *Even to give to each man according to his ways,*
> *According to the results of his deeds."*
>
> *(Jeremiah 17:10)*

BEING LOST

With these sobering vistas of the human heart and soul before us, we must ask, What does it mean to be lost? For a ruined soul is a *lost* soul. To be lost means to be *out of place*, to be omitted. *Gehenna*, the term often used in the New Testament for the place of the lost, may be thought of as the cosmic dump for the irretrievably lost and useless.

The blind pride of putting oneself at the center of the universe is the hinge upon which the entire world of the ruined self turns. When we are lost to God, we are also lost to ourselves. John Calvin said, "The surest source of destruction to men is to obey themselves."[3] Yet self-obedience seems the only reasonable path. He continued, "So blindly do we all rush in the direction of self-love, that every one thinks he has a good reason for exalting himself and despising all others in comparison."[4] Calvin would find today's scene familiar.

We must know that the ruined soul is not a person who has missed a few theological points and may flunk a theological exam at the end of life. Hell is not an "oops!" or a slip. One does not miss heaven by a hair but *by constant effort to avoid and escape God*. Further, spiritual formation is not something that may be added to the gift of eternal life as an *option*. Rather, it is the path that the eternal kind of life—the life given over to God's kingdom—naturally takes. The apostle John said, "Believing in him we have life in his name" (John 20:31, PAR). And Paul later instructed that those "in Christ"—that is, those caught up in his life and in what he is doing by the inward gift of birth from above—"are of a new making. The 'old stuff' no longer matters. It is the new that counts" (2 Corinthians 5:17, PAR).

THE NECESSITY OF REMORSE

To prosecutors and judges in our court system, as well as to people in ordinary situations of life, it still matters greatly whether wrongdoers show signs of remorse—seem to be truly sorry for what they have done. Why is that? It is because genuine remorse tells us something very deep about the individual. The person who can harm others and feel no remorse is, indeed, a different kind of person from the one who is sorry. There is little hope for genuine change in one who is without remorse, without the *anguish* of regret.

There is little remorse—or repentance—before God today, even in the church. Yet only God can deliver us from the radical evil in our heart, body, and soul. It is common to hear Christians talk of their "brokenness." But when you listen closely, you often discover that they are talking about their *wounds*, the things they have suffered, not about the evil that is in them.

Yet heartfelt remorse is the first step back from the precipice of our lostness. Without this realization of our utter ruin and helplessness before God—and without the genuine redirecting of our lives that bitter realization naturally gives rise to—*no clear path to inner transformation can be found*. This will become clearer as we look into the radical goodness of the transformed self.

Questions for Meditation and Response

1. What's the point of thinking deeply about the ruined state of your heart and soul?

2. How can God be dangerous and still love you?

3. Go back through the text and Bible passages in this chapter and write a list of the sinful qualities you struggle with. Then reflect on the past couple of weeks and add any other sinful habits of thought, action, or speech that come to mind. Add major sins of omission—times when you didn't do something loving, generous, or forgiving that you should have done.

   Pray over this list. Offer it to God at the throne of grace (see Hebrews 4:14-16).

4. When you contemplate your sins, what thoughts and feelings go through your mind? For instance:

   • I'm not that bad.
   • So-and-so is far worse than I am.

- I'm hopeless. I can't change.
- God must hate me and be so frustrated with me for being like this. I don't even want to think about him.
- I should be able to stop this and be a better person.
- This is so much a part of me that I can't imagine being different. This is who I am.
- I'm worthless. Why does God even bother with me?
- I can't bear looking at a list of my sins. It's overwhelming.
- Reading this makes me want to _____.
- I am so sad when I think about my sin.
- This has to change—I'll do whatever it takes.
- I don't feel much when I look at this list.
- Other: _____

5. Where do you see denial at work in your life?

6. Whom do you trust to hear all or part of your list? If you can't think of anyone, what can you do about that?

7. Meditate on Exodus 20:2-3 or Hebrews 4:12-16.

Restoration of the Soul

*Such were some of you; but you were washed, but
you were sanctified, but you were justified in the
name of the Lord Jesus Christ and in the Spirit
of our God.*

1 CORINTHIANS 6:11

One of the amazing things about human beings is their capacity
for restoration—a restoration that makes them somehow more
magnificent because they have been ruined. This is a strange but
hopeful thought that will become clearer as we proceed. For now,
we want to see what goes on within the person who has "returned
from ruin." So the question before us is this: What is the essential
shift (given God's work of regeneration and forgiveness) that can
lead to the reordering of the six dimensions of the human self?

The key to understanding this reordering is provided by what
we learned about human ruin in the previous chapter. John Calvin
remarked, "For as the surest source of destruction to men is to
obey themselves, so the only haven of safety is to have no other
will, no other wisdom, than to follow the Lord wherever he leads.
Let this, then, be the first step, to abandon ourselves, and devote
the whole energy of our minds to the service of God."[1] With these

words, he simply restated the basic point of view of Christ's people through the ages.[2]

Calvin continued to explain,

> *By service, I mean not only that which consists in verbal obedience, but that by which the mind, divested of its own carnal feelings, implicitly obeys the call of the Spirit of God. This transformation (which Paul calls the renewing of the mind, Romans 12:2; Ephesians 4:23), though it is the first entrance of life, was unknown to all the philosophers. They give the government of man to reason alone. . . . But Christian philosophy bids her give place, and yield complete submission to the Holy Spirit, so that the man himself no longer lives, but Christ lives and reigns in him (Galatians 2:20).*[3]

SELF-DENIAL

Calvin used the term "self-denial" to summarize the entire Christian life.[4] Self-*denial* must never be confused with self-*rejection*. If we think of our self as a toddler, self-rejection would say, "You are a disgusting, worthless child." Self-denial simply says, "No, you may not have chocolate ice cream for dinner."

Self-denial is an overall, settled condition of life in the kingdom of God, perhaps better described as "death to self." In this alone lies the key to the soul's restoration. *Spiritual formation rests on the indispensable foundation of death to self and cannot proceed*

unless that foundation is firmly laid and constantly sustained.

But what is this "self-denial" or "death to self" that goes hand in hand with restoration of the soul and, increasingly, of the whole person? At first it sounds like some dreadfully negative thing that aims to annihilate us. And, frankly, from the point of view of the ruined soul, self-denial is every bit as brutal as it seems on first approach. The ruined life is not to be enhanced but replaced. We must completely *lose* our life—our *ruined* life that is headed in the wrong direction. "Those who have found their life shall lose it," Jesus said, "while those who have lost their life for my sake shall find it" (Matthew 10:39, PAR). And again, "Whoever aims to save their life shall lose it, but whoever loses their life for my sake shall find it. For whatever you might gain by possessing the entire world, in the process you will forfeit your life—you lose your soul. What would you trade your very soul for?" (Matthew 16:25-26; Mark 8:35-36; Luke 9:24-25, PAR).

LOSING OUR LIFE TO FIND IT

When Jesus says we must lose our life to find it, he means we must give up the project of making ourselves and our survival the ultimate reference point in our world. We are foolish to treat ourselves as God should be treated. In line with this, Paul said, "Covetousness is idolatry" (Colossians 3:5, PAR). Isn't that somewhat exaggerated? No. Covetousness is self-idolatry, for it makes *our* desires paramount. To defeat covetousness, we must learn to rejoice when others enjoy the benefits they do.

57

The poet William Ernest Henley said, "I am the master of my fate: I am the captain of my soul." But when Jesus says those who find their soul will lose it, he means those who think they are in control of their life will one day find that they definitely are not in control. Instead, they are totally at the mercy of forces beyond them and even within them. They are on a sure course toward disintegration and powerlessness, toward *lostness* both to themselves and to God.

But if in remorse and repentance they give up doing only what they want—if they give up their attempt to be the ultimate reference point in their life—there is hope. If they *choose* to lose their life in favor of God's life—for the sake of Jesus and his ongoing world revolution of character—then their soul (their life) will be preserved and given back to them.

DOING WHAT YOU WANT — GOD'S WAY

What does it mean to have your life given back to you? It means that for the first time you will be able to do what you want. You will find that you actually *want* to be truthful and transparent and helpful and sacrificially loving, and you'll do it with joy. Your life will be caught up in God's life. You will *want* the good and be able to do it—which is the only true human freedom. The mind set on the Spirit's will is "life and peace" (Romans 8:6). It lives from God, and by "sowing into the Spirit, out of the Spirit reaps the eternal kind of life" (Galatians 6:8, PAR).

So life as it is normally understood, in which the objective is to secure ourselves, promote ourselves, and indulge ourselves, is to be set aside. This shift is of utmost importance to those who would enter Christian spiritual formation.

"Can I still *think* about such things?" you may ask. Yes, you can. But you increasingly won't. And as formation in Christlikeness progresses, when you do, these things simply won't matter. In fact, they will seem ridiculous and uninteresting. Instead, Jesus' words will become fresh for you. When he urges you to consider the worry-free life of the flowers and birds (see Luke 12:13-34) and to give up your anxiety about what may happen to you, his admonitions will seem obviously sane and right, whereas previously they sounded crazy, impractical, or "out of touch with reality."

TAKING THE CROSS

The same paradoxical tone applies to Jesus' teaching about who can be his disciple or apprentice. This, too, is put in very shocking language: "If you come to me," he says, "and do not prefer me over (do not 'hate') your own father, mother, wife, children, brothers and sisters—yes, and your very own life (soul)—you cannot be my apprentice" (Luke 14:26, PAR).

And then he uses an absolutely startling image—one all too familiar to his hearers but rather hard for us to appreciate fully today. It is that of a man carrying on his back the lumber that would be used to kill him when he arrived at the place of execution. Jesus says, "Whoever does not come after me carrying his own cross cannot be my apprentice" (Luke 14:27, PAR).

The cross is an instrument of death—the way of "losing your life." The teaching here is exactly the same as in the statements about losing and finding our life. It is one of the "costs." Those who are not genuinely convinced that the only real bargain in life is surrendering themselves to Jesus and his cause *cannot* learn the other lessons Jesus has to teach. They simply cannot proceed toward anything like total spiritual transformation.

But one of the great dangers in spiritual formation is that self-denial or "death to self" can be taken as but one more technique. Practices of mortification can become exercises in self-righteousness. How often practices of self-flagellation have sprung up in the history of the church! Such dreary and deadly forms of "self-denial" can be avoided only if the primary fact of our inner being is a loving vision of Jesus and his kingdom.

We may get the impression that "counting the cost" of following Jesus is discovering how terrible and painful that cost is. But to count the cost is to take into consideration both the losses and the gains of all possible courses of action and to see which is most beneficial. Jesus knew that the trials of apprenticeship (discipleship) would appear to be the only reasonable path. As has been said, "He is no fool who gives up what he cannot keep to gain what he can never lose." The cost of *non*discipleship is then seen for what it is—unbearable. That is why we become able to sustain cheerfully the *much smaller* "cost of discipleship" to Jesus.

THE CROSS AND THE CALL TO THE GREATER LIFE

Jesus came proclaiming access to the kingdom of God: the experience of God's care and supervision, available to all who trust in Christ. "Repent, for life in the kingdom of the heavens is now available to you," he said (Matthew 4:17, PAR). His presence among us—his actions and teachings—manifested and explained the kingdom. He won disciples by showing them the kingdom and inviting them to it by touching their hearts. He changed their vision of reality and their intentions for life.

Consider one of Jesus' "parables of the kingdom": "The kingdom of the heavens is like a treasure hidden in a field, which a man found and then concealed. He was ecstatic. He sold everything he had and bought the field" (Matthew 13:44, PAR).

Imagine that you discover gold or oil in a certain property and no one else knows about it. Can you see yourself being sad and feeling deprived for having to gather all your resources and "sacrifice" them in order to buy that property? Hardly! Now you know what it is like to deny yourself, take up your cross, and follow Jesus.

The self-denial Jesus speaks of is always the surrender of a lesser, dying self for a greater, eternal one—the person God intended when he created you. Confidence in this gives the occasion of "greatly rejoicing, with joy unspeakable and full of glory" (1 Peter 1:8, PAR). Jesus does not deny us personal fulfillment but shows us the only true way to it. In him we "find our life." He would prevent us from selling our birthright as creatures made in God's image—a birthright of genuine goodness, sufficiency, and power for which we are fitted by nature—for a mere bowl of soup (see Genesis 25:30-31). Each of us must examine what our bowl of soup is: perhaps illicit sex, money, position, power, seeking a reputation for deeper spirituality, and so forth. But these are "the pleasures of sin for a season."

Our "cross" of self-denial must be laid upon all our obsessive desires so that God's *agape* love can well up and flow through us. This love integrates us as whole persons and reaches out toward God and other people. This love of God is our joy. Jesus was not some harsh ascetic who practiced or imposed pain for its own sake. He did not choose death because it was good in itself, but "for the joy that was set before him, he endured the cross and despised the shame" (Hebrews 12:2, PAR).

PERFECT JOY

In chapter 8 of *The Little Flowers of Saint Francis*, Francis gives his friend Leo a teaching about what "perfect joy" is. They are trudging through the snow from Perugia to the home of their group at Saint Mary of the Angeles. Francis says that for their brotherhood to give a great example of holiness and edification in all lands would *not* be perfect joy. Nor would a great ministry of healing and raising the dead. Nor would possession of all languages and all science, nor all understanding of prophecy and Scripture and insight into the secrets of every soul. Nor would even the conversion of all unbelievers to faith in Christ!

By this point brother Leo is amazed, and he begs Francis to teach him "wherein is perfect joy." Francis's reply is that if when they come to their quarters dirty, wet, and exhausted from hunger, they are rejected, repeatedly rebuffed, and finally driven away by force, then "if we accept such injustice, such cruelty, and such contempt with patience, without being ruffled and without murmuring," and "if we bear all these injuries with patience and joy, thinking of the sufferings of our Blessed Lord, which we would share out of love for Him, write, O Brother Leo, that here, finally, is perfect joy."[5]

SUPPORTED IN THE KINGDOM

Saint Francis's perspective may seem hopelessly out of reach for us. But don't dismiss it too quickly—for very little of the Christian life works in theory, but rather only in practice. It must be tried by faith.

Of course, in laying down our life, we must experience much more than our own strength and power. In our strength, we cannot live this kingdom life. Further, there is the danger of falling into the same kind of cheery falseness that characterizes so much current talk of self-esteem. But the resources we need are abundantly supplied by Jesus through the reality of the kingdom of God. He makes this available to us *in response to our active confidence in him.*

Only with this support can we live by Jesus' teaching, "Give, and it will be given to you. They will pour into your lap a good measure—pressed down, shaken together, and running over" (Luke 6:38). For there will be periods of time when, from the human point of view, our lap is empty—when we experience the cross and tomb, but resurrection is not yet. We must then know with assurance the reality of Paul's words that "God loves a cheerful giver" and that he "is able to make all grace abound to you, so that always having all sufficiency in everything, you may have an abundance for every good deed" (2 Corinthians 9:7-8).

Jesus' resurrected presence with us assures us of God's care for all who let him be God to them and let him care for them. He tells us, "Do not be afraid, little flock, for your Father has chosen gladly to give you the kingdom" (Luke 12:32). It is the love of God and the experience of his greatness and goodness that free us from the burden of "looking out for ourselves."

What remarkable changes this introduces into our day-to-day life! Personally, at the beginning of my day—often before rising—I commit my day to the Lord's care. Usually I do this while meditatively praying through the Lord's Prayer, and possibly the Twenty-Third Psalm as well. Then I meet everything that happens as sent or at least permitted by God. I meet it resting in the hand of his care. This helps me "do all things without grumbling or disputing" (Philippians 2:14) because I have already "placed God in charge" and am trusting him to manage things for my good. I no longer have to manage the weather, airplanes, and other people.

DEAD TO SELF

As we keep before us the clear and forceful vision of Jesus and his kingdom, we make daily progress. Our personality becomes increasingly reorganized around God. Our self-denial moves beyond tentative and intermittent acts to a settled disposition and character.

At first, we must very self-consciously deny ourselves. We must work to reject the preeminence of what we want, when we want it. But when we do this, we discover surprisingly specific motions of God's grace in and around us to guide and strengthen us in our attempts at self-denial.

We will also need a wise and constant use of the spiritual disciplines, which we will explore in depth in later chapters. The disciplines are crucial because the substance of our selves—formed in a world against God—is always ready to act contrary to him in all of its dimensions. Our very habits of thinking, feeling, and willing are wrongly poised.

The one who is dead to self will not even notice some things that others would: for example, things such as social slights, verbal put-downs and innuendos, or physical discomforts. It's true, of course, that we will still notice—often quite clearly—many other rebuffs to "the dear self," as the philosopher Immanuel Kant called it. However, if we are dead to self to any significant degree, these rebuffs will not take control of us—not even to the point of disturbing our feelings or peace of mind. We will, as Saint Francis of Assisi said, "wear the world like a loose garment, which touches us in a few places and there lightly."

Does this mean that the person who is dead to self is without feeling? Does Christ commend the famous "apathy" of the Stoic or the Buddhist elimination of desire? Far from it. The issue is not just feeling or desire, but *right* feeling and *right* desire. Apprentices of Jesus will be deeply disturbed about many things and will passionately desire many things, but they will be largely indifferent to the fulfillment of their own desires as such. Merely getting their way has no significance for them. It does not disturb them. They know that "God causes all things to work together for good to those who love God, to those who are called according to His purpose" (Romans 8:28).

Beyond Anger, Retaliation, and Unforgiveness

To accept—with confidence in God—that we do not immediately have to have our way releases us from the great pressures of anger, unforgiveness, and the "need" to retaliate. This by itself is a huge transformation of the landscape of our life. It removes the root of the greater part of human evil we have to deal with in our world.[6]

Therefore, Paul directed the Christians in Thessalonica to "see that no one repays another with evil for evil, but always seek after that which is good for one another and for all people" (1 Thessalonians 5:15). Jesus commanded his hearers not to "resist him who is evil; but whoever slaps you on your right cheek, turn to him the other also" (Matthew 5:39, PAR). And Peter calls us to follow Jesus in "not returning evil for evil or insult for insult, but giving a blessing instead; for you were called for the very purpose that you might inherit a blessing" (1 Peter 3:9).

These remarkable teachings, which do so much to immediately transform life, all presuppose that one has laid down the burden of having one's own way. We can't even begin to understand them, much less follow them, except from a posture of self-denial. And this posture must be firmly supported by the confidence and experience of God's all-sufficient presence in our life.

To step with Jesus onto the path of self-denial immediately breaks the ironclad grip of sin over human personality and opens the way to an ever-fuller restoration of radical goodness to the soul. It opens us to incredible, supernatural strength for life. And because we must be active agents in this progression "from strength to strength" (Psalm 84:7), it is crucial that we now seek to understand the three main components of the process of spiritual transformation.

Questions for Meditation and Response

1. What is self-denial? Take time to reflect on and write about what it is and isn't.

2. How do you respond to the idea of self-denial? What thoughts and feelings (perhaps conflicting) arise when you think about it?

3. Give some examples of what self-denial could have looked like in your life in the past week. What would you have thought, said, and done?

4. How does one develop a habit of self-denial?

5. List arguments for and against acquiring a habit of self-denial.

6. Honestly, do you want to acquire this habit? Write a prayer to God, telling him why you do or don't.

7. Meditate on Matthew 16:25-26.

Christ's Pattern for Spiritual Transformation

But we all, with unveiled face, beholding as in a mirror the glory of the Lord, are being transformed into the same image from glory to glory, just as from the Lord, the Spirit.

2 CORINTHIANS 3:18

CHANGE *IS* POSSIBLE

It is a fearful fact that in the early stages of our spiritual development, we cannot endure seeing our inner life as it really is. Denial and self-deception are things God allows us, in part to protect us until we begin to seek him. Like the face of the mythical Medusa, our true condition away from God would turn us to stone if we ever fully confronted it. It would drive us mad. God helps us come to terms with our true condition in ways that will not destroy us outright.

Through the gentle but rigorous process of inner transformation, initiated and sustained by the graceful presence of God, we can face ourselves. And we find that change *is* possible. The change of personality clearly spelled out in the Bible and illustrated

69

throughout Christian history is possible and sought for us by God. In this chapter, we will unpack the remarkably practical pattern of transformation that Christ offers to those who seek him.

First, let's stop for a moment and summarize. So far, we've examined the basic dimensions of the human self, and we've explored the reasons for the self's dysfunction (in essence, self-worship). We've also looked at the crucial first step toward the self's restoration (the path of self-denial). We've seen that spiritual formation is God's grace-filled process by which a person moves from self-worship to Christ-centered self-denial as an increasingly steady disposition of the heart.

In the chapters to come, we will deal with each of the dimensions of our self in turn. But before we approach these practical aspects, we must notice who is at work in this move from the life of self-adulation to the one of self-denial.

WE ARE NEVER ON OUR OWN

As apprentices to Jesus, we must be active in the process of our salvation and transformation into Christlikeness. This is an inescapable fact of the gospel. But the *initiative* in the process is always God's. And here's the good news: That initiative is not something we are waiting upon. The ball is in our court. God has invaded human history and reality. Jesus Christ has died on our behalf, has risen, and is now supervising events on earth toward an end that he will certainly bring to pass, to the glory of God. The issue now concerns what *we* will do. The idea that we can do nothing toward our transformation is an unfortunate confusion of our time, and those who sponsor it never practice it, thank goodness.

If we—through well-directed and unrelenting action—effectually receive the grace of God in salvation and transformation, we certainly will be incrementally changed toward inward Christlikeness. And the transformation of our outer life, especially our behavior, will follow suit. That, too, is an escapable fact: "No good tree produces bad fruit" (Luke 6:43, PAR).

The transformation of our inner being is as much a gift of God's grace as is our justification. (Justification is our being "made right" with God—forgiven and wholly adopted by God—through faith in Christ and his work on the cross.) Of course, neither justification nor transformation is completely passive. (We will discuss the technical term *sanctification* in a later chapter.) To be forever lost, you need only *do nothing*—just stay your course. But with reference to both justification and transformation, boasting is excluded by the law of grace through faith (see Romans 3:27-31; Ephesians 2:1-10). In fact, we consume the most grace when we attempt to lead a holy life and so are constantly upheld by grace. The other option, so often taken today, is to continue in sin and simply seek or count on repeated forgiveness.

THE GENERAL PATTERN OF PERSONAL GROWTH

In any effort toward personal growth, there is a *general pattern* that is effective, and we will find the same is true for spiritual formation. Whether we are learning to play a musical instrument or speak a foreign language, our degree of success in these efforts will depend on the degree to which we understand and pursue this general pattern.

(The General PATTERN)

mmm

Let's begin with an illustration of the pattern. A well-known example is the approach to personal transformation provided by Alcoholics Anonymous and similar 12-step programs. Here, of course, the significance of the transformation is far greater than in the case of learning a language. Further, the outcome is avoiding something negative. That is, the aim of AA is to refrain from doing something very harmful, something that could possibly lead to untimely death. But the pattern is basically the same as for a positive path of personal growth.

First, we *envision* a desirable state of being or the accomplishment of a skill. Second, we actualize the *intention* to realize that state of being or skill through a decision. Third, we apply certain specific *means* to fulfill the intention and produce the desirable state of being that we envision. In the case of AA, the state of being is abstinence from alcohol and a life of sobriety. The traditional *means* of the famous twelve steps are highly effective in bringing about personal transformation. And one of these means is the conscious involvement of God in the person's life.

Ouch—Yet True!

\\ — //

Historically, the AA program was closely aligned with the church and Christian traditions. Now, it has much to give back to a church that has largely lost its grip on spiritual formation as a standard path of Christian life. The AA program works because of its awareness of the essential structure of the human self revealed in the Bible. *Any successful plan for spiritual formation, whether*

for the individual or group, will be significantly similar to the Alcoholics Anonymous program.

VIM: THE RELIABLE PATTERN

With this illustration of AA before us, the general pattern of personal transformation should now be clear. Notice that this is the pattern for all human accomplishment. Of course, spiritual formation in the Christian tradition can occur only at the initiative and the constant direction of the upholding grace of God. To keep the general pattern in mind, we will use the acronym VIM, as in the phrase "vim and vigor." VIM stands for:

- Vision
- Intention
- Means

"Vim" is a derivative of the Latin term *vis*, meaning direction, strength, force, vigor, power, energy, or virtue. Sometimes it means sense, import, nature, or essence. Spiritual formation in Christlikeness is all of this. It is the path by which we can truly, as Paul told the Ephesians, "be empowered in the Lord and in the energy of his might" (Ephesians 6:10, PAR) and "become mighty with his energy through his Spirit entering into the inward person" (Ephesians 3:16, PAR).

If we are to be spiritually formed in Christ, we must implement the appropriate *vision, intention,* and *means*. Not just any path we take will do. If this VIM pattern is not put in place properly and held there, Christ simply will not be formed in us.

THE VISION OF LIFE IN THE KINGDOM

If we are concerned about our spiritual formation and that of others, the vision of the kingdom is the place we must start. It is the place where Jesus started. That was the gospel he preached. He came announcing, manifesting, and teaching the availability and nature of the kingdom of the heavens. "For I was sent for this purpose," he said (Luke 4:43). That is simply a fact, and if we are faithful to it, if we do justice to it in full devotion, we will find our feet firmly planted on the path of Christian spiritual formation.

The kingdom of God is the range of God's effective will, where what God wants done is done.[1] It is, like God himself, "from everlasting to everlasting" (Psalm 103:17; see also Psalm 93:1-2; Daniel 4:3; 7:14). The planet Earth and its immediate surroundings seem to be the only places in creation where God permits his will to *not* be done. Therefore we pray, "Thy kingdom come, Thy will be done, on earth as it is in heaven," and hope for the time when that kingdom will be completely fulfilled even here on earth (see Luke 21:31; 22:18). The kingdom is in fact already present (see Luke 17:21; John 18:36-37) and available to those who seek it with all their hearts (see Matthew 6:13; 11:12; Luke 16:16). For those who seek the kingdom, it is true even now that "all things work together for their good" (Romans 8:28, PAR), and that nothing can cut them off from God's inseparable love and effective care (see Romans 8:35-39). That is the nature of a life in the kingdom of the heavens now.

The vision that underlies spiritual transformation into Christlikeness is the vision of life now and forever in the range of God's effective will. That is, we *partake* of the divine nature (see 2 Peter 1:4; 1 John 3:1-2) through a birth "from above" and *participate* by our actions in what God is doing now in our lifetime on earth. Therefore, we can say, "Whatever we do, speaking or acting, we do all on behalf of the Lord Jesus, giving thanks through him to God the Father" (Colossians 3:17, PAR). In everything we do on earth, we are permitted to do his work. What we are aiming for in this vision is to live fully in the kingdom of God *here* and *now*, not just hereafter.

This is a vision of life that cannot come to us naturally, though the human soul-depths automatically cry out for something like it. From time to time, our deepest thinkers, visionaries, and artists capture aspects of it.[2] It is a vision that has to be *given* to humanity by God himself in a revelation suited to our condition. We cannot clearly see it on our own. And that revelation has been given through his covenant people on earth, the Jews, with the fullest flowering of the covenant people being Jesus himself.

Jesus was prepared for through centuries of rich—though often painful—experience among the Jews. Through him the Jews have fulfilled their God-given responsibility and blessing of being a light to all the peoples of the earth (see Genesis 18:18; 22:18; Isaiah 42:1-6; 60:3). Through them all the nations of the earth are blessed—and will be even more blessed in the future.

THE INTENTION TO BE A KINGDOM PERSON

The vision of life in the kingdom through reliance upon Jesus makes it possible for us to *intend* to live in the kingdom as he did.

We can actually *decide to do it.* Of course, that means first of all to trust him, to rely on him, to count on him being the Anointed One, the Christ. It is through him that the revelation and the gift of the kingdom come to us. If we do not count on him as "the One," we will have no adequate vision of kingdom life and no way to enter it. He is "the door" and "the way."

Concretely, we live in the kingdom of God by intending to obey the example and teachings of Jesus. This is the form that *trust* in him takes. It does not take the form of merely believing things about him, however true they may be. Indeed, no one can actually believe the truth about him without intending to obey him. It is a mental impossibility. To think otherwise is to indulge a widespread illusion that now smothers spiritual formation among professing Christians.

Gandhi, who had looked closely at Christianity as practiced around him in Great Britain, remarked that if only Christians would live according to their belief in the teachings of Jesus, everyone would become Christian. We know what he meant, and he was right in that. But the dismaying truth is that the Christians *were* living according to their "belief" in the teachings of Jesus. They didn't believe them!

The idea that you can trust Christ for the hereafter but have no intention to obey him now is an illusion generated by a widespread unbelieving "Christian culture." In fact, you can no more trust Jesus and not intend to obey him than you can trust your doctor and not intend to follow his or her advice. If you don't intend to follow the advice, you simply don't trust the person.

INTENTION INVOLVES DECISION

An intention is brought to completion only by a *decision* to carry through with the intention. We commonly find people who say they intend to do certain things that they don't do. To be fair, external circumstances may prevent them from carrying out the action. And habits deeply rooted in their lives can, for a while, thwart even a sincere intention. But if something like that is not the case, we know that they never actually *decided* to do what they *say* they intended to do. Therefore, they didn't really intend to do it. They lacked the power that intention brings into our life processes.

Procrastination is a common way in which intention is aborted, but there are many other ways. The *profession* of an intention is a primary way of negotiating one's way through life. Promises and agreements involve the profession of intentions, and these are often enough to get us what we want in our social context. But how very often in human affairs is a profession empty, even in vows to God. That is why Scripture deals with swearing and vain (empty) use of God's name at such lengths. If the genuine intention is there, the deed reliably follows.

Robust intention—with its inseparable decision—can be formed and sustained only upon the foundation of a forceful vision. The elements of VIM are mutually reinforcing. Those whose word "is their bond" or "is as good as gold" are people with a vision of integrity. They "mean what they say." This is greatly valued before God, who hates "swearing falsely" and honors those "who stand by their oath even when it harms them" (Psalm 15:4, PAR). Similarly, it is the vision of life in God's kingdom that provides an adequate foundation for the steadfast intention to obey Christ.

MEANS

The vision and the solid intention to obey Christ will naturally lead to seeking out and applying the means to that end. The means of spiritual transformation are for replacing the inner character that is "lost" with the inner character of Jesus—his vision, understanding, feelings, decisions, and nature. In the attempt to find such means, we are not left to ourselves. We have rich resources available to us in the example and teachings of Jesus, in the Scriptures generally, and in his people.

Let's look at an example. Suppose we aim to be generous to someone who has taken away some of our money or property through legal processes. For whatever reason, this person is now asking for our help. Pure will, with gritted teeth, cannot be enough to enable us to be generous. By what *means*, then, can we become the kind of person who would be generous as Jesus is generous? If we have the vision and we intend to do it, we can certainly find and implement the means. God will help us do so.

I'll be brief in what follows because we will pursue a fuller treatment in chapters to come. We must start by discovering, by *identifying*, the thoughts, feelings, habits of will, social relations, and bodily inclinations that *prevent* us from being generous to this person. Our previous education should help us here—and perhaps it will to some extent—but nearly always it is insufficient.[3]

With a little reflection, we might discover that resentment and anger within us toward the person who needs our help are keeping our generosity withheld. And then there is justice. Ah, justice! Perhaps in the form of "I do not *owe* it to him. He has no claims on me." Or perhaps we feel the legal case that went against us and in his favor was rigged or unfair.

Or again, perhaps we believe we must secure ourselves by holding on to whatever surplus items we have. After all, we may need them. Who knows what the future holds? Or perhaps we think giving to people what they haven't earned will corrupt their character, leading them to believe they can get something for nothing. Or perhaps it is simply not our habit to give to people with no prior claim on us—even if they have not injured or deprived us. Or perhaps our friends, including our religious friends, would think we are fools. And so forth.

What a thicket of lostness stands in the way of doing a simple good thing! But this is the all-too-customary way of thinking and feeling. And truthfully, it is unlikely that we can do *in the moment of need* the good thing that Jesus commands.

When my neighbor who has triumphed over me in the past now stands before me in need, I will not be able to help him "on the spot." My inner being, filled with all the thoughts, feelings, and habits that characterize the ruined soul, keeps me from acting. If I intend to obey Jesus Christ, I must decide to become the kind of person who *would* obey. That is, I must find the means of changing my inner being until it is substantially like his, pervasively characterized by his thoughts, feelings, habits, and relationship with the Father.

79

Training "Off the Spot"

Not all the means for this new character are *directly* under my control. Some are the actions of God toward me and in me. But some *are* directly under my control.

I can, in moments not "on the spot," retrain my thinking by study and meditation on Christ himself and on the teachings of Scripture about God, his world, and my life. I can especially examine the teachings of Jesus in the Gospels, further elaborated by the rest of the Bible. I can also help my thinking and my feelings by deep reflection on the nature and bitter outcome of *the standard human way* in such situations—in contrast to the way of Jesus. Further, I can consciously practice self-sacrificial actions in other less demanding situations. I can become a person for whom "looking out for number one" is not the framework of my life.

I can meditate upon the lives of well-known "saints," who have practiced Jesus' way with adversaries and those in need. I can take a close look at the bitter world of legal adversaries—at how people learn to hate one another in court—to see if I want to be a part of *that*. I can earnestly pray that God will work in my inner being to change the things that keep me from obeying his Son. And many other things can be done as *means* to fulfilling the vision of life in God that I intend and have chosen.

So we come back in a different way to the statement, "Where there is a will, there is a way." It turns out to be true here, because God is involved and helps those who seek him. The entire VIM of Christ's life is also available to us to the point where, with practice, a life of obedience to Christ actually "comes naturally."

We are inwardly and outwardly transformed.

In future chapters, we will turn to some of the things we can do with God's assistance in *each* of the dimensions of our life on our path toward a revolution of character. Our goal will be to progressively form our inner, hidden world so that "the tree is good" to the farthest reaches of root and branch.

Questions for Meditation and Response

1. Begin by praying for a clear and rich vision of your life in God's kingdom here and now. It might be helpful to meditate on Matthew 6:9-13.

2. Describe your present vision of what your life in God's kingdom can be. What would you think, feel, and do?

3. Deepen your vision by meditating on Romans 8:28-39 and 1 John 3:1-2.

4. What questions do you have about the kingdom that would give you a clearer vision of it? Write them down and then ask God to lead you to answers in the Scriptures or from someone more mature in following Christ.

5. How do you respond to this statement: "The idea that you can trust Christ for the hereafter but have no intention to obey him now is an illusion generated by a widespread unbelieving 'Christian culture'"? What are the implications?

6. Why is it ineffective to practice the spiritual disciplines without a clear and settled intention to obey the example and teachings of Jesus?

7. Where are you right now regarding such an intention? Think about the means sketched in this chapter—are you willing to undergo such a process?

   If possible, schedule half a day to make the decision to increasingly become a kingdom person. That will give you time to fully dedicate yourself to the decision and carefully weigh how your other life priorities will be affected. You might want to schedule your half day to come shortly after you've finished reading this book.

Chapter 6

The Battle for
Our Thought Life

I have set the LORD continually before me;
Because He is at my right hand, I will not be
shaken.

PSALM 16:8

THE FIRST MOVE BACK FROM RUIN

We first turned away from God in our thoughts, so it is in our thought life that we must ignite the revolution of our character. Thoughts are where we can begin to truly change. In our thoughts dwell powerful ideas, images, and information—and these three things will become crucial in our pursuit of spiritual transformation.

The ultimate freedom we have as human beings is the power to choose what we let our mind dwell on. We are not totally free in this respect, of course, because we are "dead in trespasses and sins." But we do have the ability and the responsibility *to try to retain God in our mind*—if only in an inadequate and halting manner. If we do this, we will surely make progress toward him. For when we truly seek God as best we can, he—who always knows what is in our heart—will make himself known to us. It is because of this fact that human beings always remain responsible before God, even those who are spiritually dead.

IDEAS AND IMAGES IN SPIRITUAL FORMATION

A battle is raging for our mind. The apostle Paul warned us that "our struggle is not against flesh and blood, but against the rulers, against the powers, against the world forces of this darkness, against the spiritual forces of wickedness in the heavenly places" (Ephesians 6:12). These higher-level powers and forces are spiritual agencies that primarily work within the idea systems of our culture.

Idea systems are generally held assumptions about reality. They are patterns of thinking and interpretation, historically developed and socially shared. Examples of ideas are freedom, education, happiness, "the American dream," science, progress, death, home, the feminine or masculine, the religious, "Christian," "Muslim," church, democracy, fairness, justice, family, evolution, God, and the secular. Ideas such as these are so pervasive and essential to how we approach life that we often do not even know they are there or understand how they work. Our particular idea system is a cultural artifact, growing up with us from earliest childhood out of the teachings, expectations, and observable behaviors of family and community. These idea systems can be manipulated by evil forces; they are, in fact, evil's main tool for dominating humanity.

By contrast, we who have been rescued "from the power of darkness and transferred . . . into the kingdom of his beloved Son" (Colossians 1:13, NRSV) are to "let this mind be in [us], which was also in Christ Jesus" (Philippians 2:5, KJV). This is an essential way of describing the substance, the underlying reality, of Christian spiritual formation. We are, in Paul's familiar language, transformed precisely by the "renewing of our mind" (Romans 12:2, PAR).

Closely associated with these idea systems are *images* that occupy our mind. Images are always concrete and specific, as opposed to the abstractness of ideas, and they are heavily laden with feeling. They frequently have a powerful emotional and sensuous linkage to governing idea systems.

For example, hair (long, short, skinhead, green, orange, or purple), body piercings, tattoos, flags (and their desecration), and clothing styles have provided powerful images and symbols for conflicting idea systems. These images are often adopted by one generation, ethnic group, or locale to set itself off from another.

Of course, Jesus understood the great significance of images. He carefully selected an image that brilliantly conveys himself and his message: the cross. The cross represents the lostness of man as well as the sacrifice of God and the abandonment to God that brings redemption. No doubt it is the all-time most powerful image and symbol of human history. Need we say he knew what he was doing in selecting it? He is the Master of images. For their own benefit, his followers need to keep the image of the cross vividly present in their mind.

OUR IMAGE OF GOD

This is the basic idea behind all temptation: God is seen as depriving us of what is good by his commands, so we imagine that we must take matters into our own hands and act contrary to what he has said. This image of God leads to our pushing him out of our thoughts and putting ourselves on the throne of the universe. The condition of the ruined soul and ruined world naturally results. *The single most important thing in our mind is our idea of God and the associated images.* A. W. Tozer did not exaggerate when he said,

> *That our idea of God corresponds as nearly as possible to the true being of God is of immense importance to us. Compared with our actual thoughts about Him, our creedal statements are of little consequence. Our real idea of God may lie buried under the rubbish of conventional religious notions and may require an intelligent and vigorous search before it is finally unearthed and exposed for what it is. Only after an ordeal of painful self-probing are we likely to discover what we actually believe about God.*
>
> *A right conception of God is basic not only to systematic theology but to practical Christian living as well. It is to worship what the foundation is to the temple; where it is inadequate or out of plumb the whole structure must sooner or later*

im before us. When we do so, we will be assisted by
n ways far beyond anything we can understand on
the ideas and images that governed the life of Christ
thought life will possess *us*.[3]

CRUCIAL ROLE OF GOOD THINKING TODAY

ing is tremendously important for us today, as it was
. Perhaps we are in a time when it is more important
*The prospering of God's cause on earth depends upon
thinking well.*
empowered by the Holy Spirit, a straight-thinking mind
arly takes in the "information" of the Scripture is a mind
idly on the high road of spiritual formation under God.
n the Psalms:

The law of the LORD is perfect, restoring the soul;
The testimony of the LORD is sure, making wise
   the simple. . . .
The commandment of the LORD is pure,
   enlightening the eyes. (19:7-8)

Your word I have treasured in my heart,
That I may not sin against You. (119:11)

Your word is a lamp to my feet
And a light to my path. (119:105)

---

*collapse. I believe there is scarcely an error in
doctrine or a failure in applying Christian ethics
that cannot be traced finally to imperfect and
ignoble thoughts about God.*[1]

START WITH THE RIGHT INFORMATION

Information begins our transformation. Consider the words of
Romans 10:14: "How will they believe in Him whom they have
not heard?" Without correct information, our ability to think
has nothing from which to work. Indeed, without the requisite
information, we may be afraid of thinking at all or may simply be
incapable of thinking straight.

Failure to know what God is really like and what his law
requires destroys the soul, ruins society, and leads people to eternal
ruin: "My people are destroyed for lack of knowledge" (Hosea 4:6,
NRSV), and "A people without understanding comes to ruin" (4:14,
NRSV). This is the tragic condition of Western culture today, which
has put away the information about God that God himself has
made available.

The first task of Jesus in his earthly ministry was to *proclaim*
God—to *inform* those around him of the availability of eternal
life from God through Jesus himself. He made it clear that by
placing their confidence in him, by "believing on him," they could
immediately enter into the eternal life enjoyed by those in "the
kingdom of the heavens." This is basic information for human
life.

Jesus had to combat much false information about the Father and bring to light the correct "Father facts" (see Matthew 11:27; John 6:46). He showed the many ways in which God is love. This he did by *proclaiming* the immediate availability of the kingdom of God from the surrounding heavens, by *manifesting* its presence through use of its power to help people, and by *teaching* in various ways its exact nature (see Matthew 4:23; 9:35).

On the evening before his death, with his teaching ministry finished, Jesus said to his Father in prayer, "I manifested Your name to the men whom You gave Me" (John 17:6). That is, "I have made them understand what you are really like." His death was understood by his disciples to be an ultimate revelation of the Father heart of God: "God proves his love for us," Paul wrote, "in that while we were still rebelling against him, Christ died for us" (Romans 5:8, PAR). That is, his death was a revelation of the essential nature of reality. Without knowledge of its meaning, we are desperately ignorant of reality, and therefore all our thinking produces only monstrous falsehoods.

SPIRITUAL FORMATION REQUIRES THINKING

The gospel of Jesus directly repudiates all false information about God and about the meaning of human life. And it works to undermine the power of those ideas and images that shift our life away from God. But for the gospel to have this effect on us, we must *use* our ability to think.

What is thinking? It is the activity of searching out what is true in light of given facts or assumptions. It extends the information we

have in our mind and enables
it clearly and wholly. And thin
ideas and images as well. It re
powerful gift of God to be used

Here is Paul, thinking unde
us, who is against us? He who
delivered Him over for us all, how
give us all things?" (Romans 8:31-

Here is Martin Luther, think
of God before his examiners at W
by Scripture and plain reason—I
popes and councils, for they have
conscience is captive to the Word o
recant anything, for to go against co
safe. God help me. Amen." The earl
statement added the famous words,
otherwise."[2]

And so we must inform our thinki
We must thoughtfully take that Word
its meaning, and explore its implications
to our own life. What are we to do in the
gospel, the revelation of God, and human
Bible? We must "pay greater attention to
that we do not drift away from it" (Hebrew
thoughtfully put Scripture into practice.

We must *seek the Lord* by devoting our
the information of the gospel and putting in
find there. This is the primary way of focusi

and setting h
God's grace
our own. An
through *his*

THE

Good think
in the past
than ever.
his people
When
that regul
placed so
We read

I love Your commandments
Above gold, yes, above fine gold.
Therefore I esteem right all Your precepts
concerning everything. (119:127-128)

Those who love Your law have great peace,
And nothing causes them to stumble. (119:165)

THOUGHT, LOVE, AND WORSHIP

When our mind increasingly dwells upon God as he is presented in his Word, we begin to love him passionately. This love in turn brings our thoughts steadily back to God. In this way, he will always be before our mind. Thomas Watson beautifully wrote long ago,

> *The first fruit of love is the musing of the mind upon God. He who is in love, his thoughts are ever upon the object. He who loves God is ravished and transported with the contemplation of God. "When I awake, I am still with thee" (Ps. 139:18). The thoughts are as travellers in the mind. David's thoughts kept heaven-road, "I am still with Thee." God is the treasure, and where the treasure is, there is the heart. By this we may test our love to God. What are our thoughts most upon? Can we say we are ravished with delight when we think on God? Have our thoughts got wings? Are they fled*

aloft? Do we contemplate Christ and glory? Oh, how far are they from being lovers of God, who scarcely ever think of God! "God is not in all his thoughts" (Ps. 10:4). A sinner crowds God out of his thoughts. He never thinks of God, unless with horror, as the prisoner thinks of the judge.[4]

In this way, we enter a life of *worship*. To think of God as he is, we cannot help but lapse into worship; and worship is the single most powerful force in completing and sustaining restoration in the whole person. Every evil tendency in every dimension of the self retreats into the shadows. We can insist: *Worship is at once the overall character of the renovated thought life and the only safe place for a human being to stand.*

An old hymn contains these lines:

In our astonished reverence we confess
Thine uncreated loveliness.

"Astonished reverence" is a good paraphrase for worship, as is that of A. W. Tozer's phrase, "admiration to the point of wonder and delight." That is the true outcome of renewal of the thought life. The first statement in the Lord's Prayer is, "Hallowed be Thy name." It is first because it is the most important one. To the extent that God is exalted in the minds of people and his very name is cherished with utmost respect, everything else goes right. You can verify this experimentally in yourself.

THE WAY FORWARD

There are no formulas in the spiritual life because it is not a life that runs on its own. It runs on interaction with God. The key to transforming this "thought" dimension of the person, however, is the VIM structure. This chapter has dealt almost exclusively with the *V* part of the structure: *vision*. The greatest need lies there. Unless the *vision* is properly grasped, the *intention* will be malformed or nonexistent and the *means* will be chaotic and ineffectual.

The intention to have our mind properly formed is to have the great God and Father of our Lord Jesus Christ a constant presence in our mind, crowding out every false idea. We must have the intention to use divinely powerful weapons "for the destruction of fortresses. We are destroying speculations and every lofty thing raised up against the knowledge of God, and we are taking every thought captive to the obedience of Christ" (2 Corinthians 10:4-5).

With the vision in place, adopting this intention is next. You may think, *I can't.* Remember, God will help you carry out your decision and form a solid intention. But he will not do it for you. Have you decided to keep God a constant presence in your mind?

Once you have the *V* and the *I* in place, you will begin to find appropriate, orderly, bearable, and effectual means to fulfill your decision to realize the vision. There are certain tried-and-true disciplines we can use to aid in the transformation of our thought life toward the mind of Christ.[5] *Spiritual disciplines are activities that are in our power and that enable us to do what we cannot do by direct effort.* We cannot transform our ideas and images, or even the information in our mind, by direct effort. But we can adopt certain practices that, by indirect action, will increasingly produce that effect.

The most obvious thing we can do is draw certain key portions of Scripture into our mind and make them a part of the permanent fixtures there. This is the primary discipline for the thought life. We need to know these passages like the back of our hand, and a good way to do that is to memorize them and then constantly turn them over in our mind as we go through the circumstances of our daily life (see Joshua 1:8; Psalm 1).

We cannot realize the desired effect by focusing on isolated verses, but it will certainly come as we ingest *passages*, such as Romans 5:1-8; 8:1-15; 1 Corinthians 13; or Colossians 3:1-17. When you take these into your mind, your mind will become filled with the light of God himself.

You may say, "I can't memorize like that." I assure you, you can. God made your mind for it, and he will help you. He *really* wants you to do this. As you choose to give your time and energy to the transformation of your mind, *it will happen!* You will discover that the mind of the Spirit is life and peace, and in every deflection of life, your mind will automatically recenter on God as the needle of a compass returns to north.

IMAGES AND SAYINGS

We also need to be in the presence of images, both visual and auditory, such as wise sayings, poetry, and songs. These can constantly direct our mind toward God, Jesus Christ, the Spirit, and the people of God. Icons have a millennia-long track record with the people of God and can be a powerful way of effortlessly keeping entire stories and teachings before the mind. We might arrange to have them tastefully present in each of our living and work spaces, so that they are always present in our visual field. We can use them to dispel destructive thoughts and to envision ourselves as before God in all levels of our being.

Not long ago, people in the United States commonly had edifying sayings on their walls. I recall from my childhood one that said, "Only one life. It will soon be past. Only what's done for Christ will last." This and other good sayings were constantly before the minds of all who lived in the house. They were effective because they became an enduring presence and influence in their minds.

Finding Others Who Are
Walking the Walk

Spiritual formation cannot be a private activity because it is a matter of whole-life transformation. You need to *seek out* others in your community who are pursuing spiritual transformation. They might be members of your family or acquaintances in a nearby congregation of Christians. If no one comes to mind, you can ask God to lead you to people who can walk with you as you walk with Christ. Then, in patience, stay with them.

This naturally leads us to include under *means* the identification of older practitioners of The Way. We need to study the lives of those who have learned how to have a transformed mind—though not necessarily in order to do exactly what they did, for they are not lawgivers, nor are they always right, much less perfect.

We are talking about *practitioners*, not theologians. Working backward in time, we find people such as Billy Graham, Teresa of Calcutta, Dawson Trotman, E. Stanley Jones, and Frank Laubach—or even longer ago, John Wesley, William Law, Martin Luther, Ignatius of Loyola, Francis of Assisi, and many others, famous or not so famous.[6] How did they come to be able to live with "the Lord always before them"? We learn from them by making them our close companions on the way. However, don't just look at what Dawson Trotman or John Wesley, for example, *accomplished*. Look at *the details of how they lived* their lives and then sensibly adapt those details to your life.

There is much more we could say on the details of the *means*. But if we take in God through his Word and walk the way of those who know by experience the transformation of the mind, that transformation will come to us and pervade every dimension of our person. *God will see to it!*

Questions for Meditation and Response

1. Why is it so important to keep God a constant presence in our mind?

2. Reflect on the idea of freedom. What messages about freedom do you get from TV ads, movies, rock lyrics, political news, or other sources? How does the idea of freedom influence your desires, feelings, and choices?

3. What are three thoughts that have occupied your mind this week? Why do you suppose those, rather than others, have come to you? How have those thoughts affected your life?

4. What images of God seem most common and influential in our world? How about in your own thinking and devotional life? In that of your friends?

5. Meditate on the cross. You could focus your thoughts on a painting or sculpture of the Crucifixion or on a Bible passage such as Mark 15:21-41.

6. Choose one of these passages to ingest—to read and think about over and over until you have memorized it: Romans 5:1-8; 8:1-15; 1 Corinthians 13; Colossians 3:1-17. Make a plan for following through on this intention, such as devoting your lunchtime for the next couple of weeks to reflection on this passage. If obstacles arise in your mind (*I can't memorize this*; *Memorizing is boring*; *I don't have time*), how can you address them?

7. Who can be your partner(s) in pursuing spiritual transformation? If no one comes to mind, start asking God to lead you to someone.

Educating Our Feelings

*For the kingdom of God is not eating and drinking,
but righteousness and peace and joy in the Holy
Spirit.*

ROMANS 14:17

*Those who belong to Christ Jesus have crucified
the flesh with its passions and desires.*

GALATIANS 5:24

THE VISION OF ONESELF
AS REALLY DIFFERENT

Feelings are central to our spiritual formation in Christ. In the revolution of our character, many of our feelings (emotions, sensations, desires) must be changed. At first you may think this is impossible. But please stay with me. I hope to show you that if a compelling vision of yourself as one who is free from enslaving feelings can possess you, then you are in a position to *give up* the negative desires or emotions you now have. The VIM pattern of change will work here as elsewhere.

Of course, achieving this new vision of oneself does not simply take a snap of the fingers. It requires genuine openness to radical change, wrestling with key hindrances, and abundant supplies of divine grace. For most people, these things come to them only after they "hit bottom" and discover their total helplessness to change in their own power. Many cannot envision who they would be without the fears, anger, lusts, power ploys, bitterness, depressive moods, and inner wounds that have imprisoned them for so long. Their identity is bound up in their habit-worn feelings.

A person enslaved in this way must give up the hours of fantasizing sensual indulgence or revenge. He must quit his domination or injury of others in attitude, word, or deed. He will not repay evil for evil, blow for blow, taunt for taunt, hatred for hatred. He will not be always on the hunt to satisfy his lust of the eyes and the pride of life (see 1 John 2:16). He must content himself with the mere identity "apprentice of Jesus." That is the starting point from which his new identity must emerge.

FEELINGS MOVE OUR LIVES — FOR GOOD OR BAD

The word *feeling* encompasses a range of things. We feel warm, hungry, restless, or fearful. Feelings include pain and pleasure, sleepiness and weariness, sexual interest and desire, loneliness and homesickness, anger and jealousy. But feelings also include comfort and satisfaction, a sense of accomplishment, intellectual curiosity, compassion for others, the enjoyment of beauty, a sense of honor, and delight in God.

Feelings *move* us, and *we enjoy being moved*. They give us a sense of being alive. Without feelings, we would have no interest in things, no inclination to action. To "lose interest in life" means we have to carry on by mere exertion of will or by waiting for things to happen. This is a condition to be dreaded, and it cannot be sustained for long. It is also why so many people become dependent upon substances and activities that give them feeling, even if the dependence harms them and those near them.

So feelings are essential to life. Healthy feelings, properly ordered, are essential to a good life. If we are to be formed in Christlikeness, we must take good care of our feelings and not just let them "happen." The one known as the Good Samaritan in the story Jesus told (see Luke 10:30-37) was distinguished from the priest and the Levite by the fact that "when he saw him [the wounded man], he felt compassion" (verse 33). This feeling of compassion is what led him to help the man and "be a neighbor to" him (verses 36-37).

Did the priest and the Levite, then, have *no* feelings? They had feelings, certainly—feelings of disdain, perhaps, or fear of harm if they became involved. Or they may have felt a sense of urgency as they remembered the business awaiting them at the end of their journey. Their self-centered feelings moved them more than did the need of this unfortunate man. They hardened their hearts to feelings of sympathy and concern.

DESTRUCTIVE FEELINGS

Many of the feelings that animate us are destructive to ourselves and to others. Jesus' younger brother, James, pointedly asked, "What is the source of quarrels and conflicts among you? Is not the source your pleasures that wage war in your members? You lust and do not have; so you commit murder. You are envious and cannot obtain; so you fight and quarrel" (4:1-2). And elsewhere he pointed out that "where jealousy and selfish ambition exist, there is disorder and every evil thing" (3:16). The cause of these conflicts is the underlying feelings involved, which, if denied or suppressed, will only break out again.

The Old Testament book of Proverbs is full of wisdom about the good and evil produced by feelings in our lives. As we have already seen, "The fear of the LORD is the beginning of wisdom" (9:10). Moreover,

Hatred stirs up strife,
But love covers all transgressions. (10:12)

When pride comes, then comes dishonor. (11:2)

Anxiety in a man's heart weighs it down. (12:25)

A cheerful heart has a continual feast. (15:15)

A joyful heart is good medicine,
But a broken spirit dries up the bones. (17:22)

He who loves pleasure will become a poor man;
He who loves wine and oil will not become rich.

(21:17)

The reward of humility and the fear of the LORD
Are riches, honor and life. (22:4)

The heavy drinker and the glutton will come to poverty,
And drowsiness will clothe one with rags. (23:21)

The fear of man brings a snare,
But he who trusts in the LORD will be exalted.

(29:25)

FEELINGS SPREAD

Much of the great power of feelings over life derives not just from the fact that they *touch* us or *move* us but from the fact that they *creep into other areas of our life*. They change the overall tone of our life. They spread like yeast or an unstable dye. They may take over everything else in us and can even determine the outcome of our life as a whole.

I recall a woman (it could just as easily have been a man) who allowed the thought that she had been treated unfairly for years in her marriage and her job to possess her. Rather than addressing the circumstances or just turning her mind away from this thought, she brooded over it. For years she did this, developing a tremendous sense of injustice and outrage. She even cultivated these feelings with the aid of sympathetic friends. This "root of bitterness" (Hebrews 12:15) gradually spread over her whole personality, seeping deeply into her body and soul. It became something you could see in her bodily motions and actions and hear oozing through the language she used. It affected her capacity to see what was actually going on around her and to realize how destructive her feelings were. She was in what Bob Mumford called "the prison of resentment," though she thought she was acting freely. This kind of destructive progression is what the education of our feelings must reverse.

THE SECRET OF ADDICTION

Abandonment to feeling—allowing oneself to be "carried away" by feeling—is actually *sought* by many on a regular basis. This is a testimony to our epidemic deadness of soul. People want to feel and to feel strongly.[1]

The opposite of peace is not war, but deadness. The "dead soul" is one waiting to explode or fall apart, one that will seek out trouble for reasons it cannot understand. In its desolate life away from God, there is no drama to provide constructive feelings that would keep life from being a burden. Such persons really have no hope. This is the key to those "lives of quiet desperation" that Thoreau attributed to "most men." They seek feeling for its own sake. But satisfaction in feeling alone always demands *stronger* feeling. It never limits itself.

This simple point is what explains the powerful grip of addiction, including the various forms of substance abuse, sexual perversion, or addiction to praise. Addiction is a phenomenon centered on feelings. The addict is one who, in one way or another, has given in to feeling of one kind or another and has placed it in the position of ultimate value in life.

IMAGES AND "MOODS"

Feelings are often sustained by ideas and images. Hopelessness and rejection (feelings of worthlessness and "not belonging") live on images—often of some specific scene or scenes of unkindness, brutality, or abuse. These scenes have become a permanent fixture within the mind, radiating negativity and leaving a background of deadly ideas that take over how we think and structure our whole world.

Such images also foster and sustain moods. What we call "moods" are simply feelings that *pervade* our selves and everything around us. They are, of course, extremely hard to do anything about, precisely because one cannot stand outside of them. Anger, fear, or pain can *become* moods because of their capacity to spread.

On the positive side, there are feelings and moods associated with confidence, worthiness, being acceptable and "belonging," purposefulness, love, hope, joy, and peace. Being "accepted in the beloved" (Ephesians 1:6, KJV) is the humanly indispensable foundation for the reconstruction of all these positive feelings, moods, and their underlying conditions.

As we pursue this reconstruction, it is essential not to confuse the condition with the accompanying feeling—peace, for example, with the feeling of peacefulness. If we confuse them, we very likely will try to manage the *feelings* and disregard or deny the reality of the *conditions*. The person who primarily wants the feeling of being loved or being "in love" will be incapable of sustaining loving relationships, whether with God or with other humans. And the person who wants the feeling of peacefulness will be unable to do the things that make for peace—especially doing what is right and confronting evil. So we must choose and act with regard to the *condition* and allow the feelings to take care of themselves, as they certainly will.

FEELINGS IN THE SPIRITUALLY TRANSFORMED PERSON

What, then, are the feelings that will dominate a life that is being inwardly transformed to be like Christ? They are the feelings associated with love, joy, and peace. These are the three fundamental dimensions of the fruit (notice the singular) of the Spirit. Love, joy, and peace express themselves as *one* fruit that also includes "patience, kindness, goodness, faithfulness, gentleness, self-control" (Galatians 5:22-23).

Faith (confidence) and hope are also very important in structuring the feeling dimension of the mind. They are focused on what is good. They are strength giving and pleasant even in the midst of pain or suffering.

HOPE AND FAITH

Hope is inseparable from joy. Hope is anticipation of a good that is not yet here. Sometimes the "good" is deliverance from an evil. Then "we are saved by hope" (Romans 8:24, PAR) and "we rejoice in hope" (12:12, PAR) because "if we hope for what we do not see, with perseverance we wait eagerly for it" (8:25). That eager anticipation strengthens us to stay faithful to God.

Hope is closely related to faith. Faith is confidence grounded in reality. As Hebrews 11:1 says, faith is "substance" and "evidence," or proof (KJV). Faith is not—as some contemporary translations have it—subjective, psychological states such as "being sure of" or "having a conviction of."

Rather, faith sees the reality of the invisible. Accordingly, Moses "left Egypt, not fearing the wrath of the king" (Hebrews 11:27). Egypt and its king were in the realm of "the seen." Moses was able to disregard them and stick with his goal because he saw the One who is invisible—*but no less real for that!* "For he endured, as seeing Him who is unseen" (verse 27). That is faith as the Bible portrays it.

THE FOUNDATION FOR A LIFE FULL OF LOVE

Romans 5:1-5 gives us remarkable insight into spiritual formation, especially as it concerns feelings. The passage outlines an instructive and inspiring progression. Initial faith in Christ gives us "our introduction by faith into this grace in which we stand" (verse 2). This is the new birth into Christ's kingdom. That new birth puts an end to the war between God and us. Once we know that God is good, we are thrilled with the hope that God's goodness will serve as the basis for our existence. Therefore, "we exult in hope of the glory of God" (verse 2).

This then opens the path for transformation of our character. We are also thrilled about our tribulations! We know that they will prove God's power and faithfulness. Trusting in him in all things becomes our settled character. Therefore, "we also exult in

our tribulations, knowing that tribulation brings about perseverance; and perseverance, proven character" (verses 3-4; compare
James 1:2-4).

Character is a matter of our entire personality and life, which
has now been transformed by the process of perseverance under
God. Hope therefore now pervades our life as a whole. And the
great marvel is that this hope "does not disappoint, because the
love of God has been poured out within our hearts through the
Holy Spirit who was given to us" (verse 5).

LOVE

Therefore, faith in Christ leads us to *stand* in the grace of God. And
standing in that grace leads to a life full of love. But what exactly
is love? Love is *willing the good*. We love something or someone
when we promote its good for its own sake. What characterizes
the deepest essence of God is love—that is, willing the good. His
very creation of the world is an expression of willing the good. It's
expected, therefore, that his world would be found by him to be
"very good" (Genesis 1:31). His love and goodwill toward humans
is not an add-on to a nature that is fundamentally careless or even
hostile. Love expresses what God always is in every respect.

God intrudes in our world gently and in many ways, but
especially in the person of Jesus Christ. It is he who stands for
love, as no one else has ever done. His crucifixion is the all-time
high-water mark of love on earth. "While we were still helpless, at
the right time Christ died for the ungodly" (Romans 5:6). No other
source, whether inside or outside of religions, even comes close to

the love that God shows in Christ. This is the first "move" of love in the process of redemption: "He first loved us" (1 John 4:19).

When we receive the revelation of God's love in Christ, that amazing love makes it possible for us to love in turn. His love awakens our love for him. Therefore, the first Great Commandment—to love God with all our being—can be fulfilled because of the beauty of God given in Christ.

At the same time, we begin to love others who love God. And when "we love one another, God abides in us, and His love is perfected in us" (1 John 4:12). The first Great Commandment makes it possible to fulfill the second Great Commandment: love of neighbor as oneself. The kingdom fellowship of Christ's apprentices is a community of love (see John 13:34-35). This is how love is made perfect or complete. And "perfect love casts out fear" (1 John 4:18).

JOY

Joy is natural in the presence of such love. Joy is a pervasive *sense* of well-being. It is not the same as pleasure, though it is pleasant. It is deeper and broader than any pleasure. Pleasure and pain are always specific to some particular object or condition, such as eating something you really like (pleasure) or recalling some really foolish thing you did (pain).

But for joy, *all* is well, even in the midst of suffering and loss. Self-sacrificial love is therefore always joyous—no matter the pain involved. For we are always looking at the larger scene in which love rules, where all things—no matter what—work together for good to those who love God and are drawn into his purposeful actions on earth (see Romans 8:28).

Joy is a basic element of inner transformation into Christlikeness. Thus when Jesus was sharing with his closest friends the events that were about to unfold on the night before his crucifixion, he left his peace with them (see John 14:27). Then, after explaining to them how he would be the vine and they the branches, constantly drawing rich life from him, he said, "These things I have spoken to you so that My joy may be in you, and that your joy may be made full" (15:11). This theme of being *full* of joy is repeated twice more in John's version of Jesus' final discourse and prayer (see 16:24; 17:13).

But here again we must not be passive. Therefore Paul, while in jail, spoke to the Philippians of his own contentment "in whatever circumstances" (Philippians 4:11) and urged them to "rejoice in the Lord always; again I will say, rejoice!" (4:4).

Peace

Peace is the calm that results from assurance about how things will turn out. We are no longer *striving*, inwardly or outwardly, to save some outcome dear to us or to avoid another.

Peace with God comes only from acceptance of his gift of life in his Son (see Romans 5:1-2). We are then assured of the outcome of our life and are no longer trying to justify ourselves before God and others. We have accepted that we are not righteous or even competent and that we cannot be so on our own.

From those around us we must simply *assume* grace and mercy, not that we will get what we deserve. We are beggars on our way through this world. Justice is not enough for our needs, and we couldn't stand it if we got it. When others do not extend the grace and mercy we need, we have to draw on the abundance in God. "Who is this who is condemning me?" we must ask ourselves and then remember, "Jesus even died for me, was raised from the dead, and is now standing up for me before God" (Romans 8:34, PAR).

SOME THINGS WE CAN DO

The revolution of character in the dimension of feeling is a matter of carefully cultivating love, joy, and peace, first by receiving them from God and from those already living in him. Then, as we grow, we can extend love, joy, and peace to others and everything around us in attitude, prayer, and action. Following our VIM pattern, we must intend these feelings and decide they will be present in all we are and do.

For many of us, just coming to honest terms with what our feelings really are will be a huge task. Paul says in Romans 12:9, "Let love be without hypocrisy." That is, let it be genuine or sincere. To do only this will require serious effort, deep learning, and quantities of grace.

To recognize the reality of our feelings and agree with the Lord to abandon the destructive ones, we may need to write out what those feelings are in a letter to the Lord. Or we may want to confer about them with a wise Christian friend who knows how to listen to us and to God at the same time.

We may ask friends or our fellowship group to pray for us. Journaling about progress with feelings can also help. It can bring to light the ideas and images or past events on which the destructive feelings are based. Those, too, will need to be replaced or revised.

We can be very sure that a life of love, joy, and peace is God's intent for us. Paul prayed for his friends in Ephesus that they would be "rooted and grounded in love" and "know the love of Christ which surpasses knowledge, that [they] may be filled up to all the fullness of God" (Ephesians 3:17-19). And we have seen the intent of Jesus: "That My joy may be in you, and that your joy may be made full" (John 15:11). He does not leave us bereft: "Peace I leave with you; My peace I give to you; not as the world gives do I give to you. Do not let your heart be troubled, nor let it be fearful" (14:27).

Questions for Meditation and Response

1. Close your eyes and imagine yourself still yourself but filled with a passionate love for God and others, a joyful sense of well-being, and confidence in how your life will turn out. Picture your face or imagine yourself entering your home or workplace with those as your dominant feelings. What expression is on your face? How do you walk? What do you say to others? Play out this imaginary scene for a few minutes. How hard is it for you to imagine this?

2. Write a letter to God expressing as well as you can your dominant feelings—your emotions, physical sensations, and desires. If possible, share this letter with a person you trust.

3. Under the subhead "The Foundation for a Life Full of Love" on page 107 is a reflection on Romans 5:1-5. Read this passage in light of that reflection. Which of the statements there do you deeply know to be true? At which ones do you get stuck? For instance, do you "exult in hope of the glory of God" (verse 2)? That is, are you thrilled with the hope that God's goodness will serve as the basis for your existence here and now? Pray slowly through this passage, asking God to show you the truth of each phrase. Journal about the ones at which you're currently stuck.

4. What do you do to deaden feelings you want to avoid or to create feelings when you're deadened? For example, are there emotions you like to trigger with television or food?

5. Meditate on God's greatness and love for you. He who not only loves you but *is* Love is so great that you live beyond harm in his hands. There is nothing that can happen to you that will not turn out for your good. *Nothing.* (See Romans 8:28.)

6. Meditate on being "accepted in the beloved" (Ephesians 1:6, KJV). Use a passage such as Luke 15:11-32; Romans 8:31-34; or Ephesians 1:3-10. What doubts do you have about being accepted? How does God respond?

Transforming Our Character

If anyone is willing to do His will, he will know of the teaching, whether it is of God or whether I speak from Myself.

JOHN 7:17

Would you know who is the greatest saint in the world? It is not he who prays most or fasts most; it is not he who gives most alms or is most eminent for temperance, chastity, or justice; but it is he who is always thankful to God, who wills everything that God wills, who receives everything as an instance of God's goodness and has a heart always ready to praise God for it.

WILLIAM LAW

MY CHARACTER IS ME

Character is that internal, overall structure of our self that reveals our long-running patterns of behavior. It is character that explains why employers use credit reports, resumes, and letters of reference—rudimentary as they may be—to make personnel decisions. These things do not just tell what someone did; they attempt to reveal what kinds of thoughts and feelings a person habitually acts from. They serve to predict how he or she will act in the future.

Our character can change. For example, domestic physical violence or verbal injury is a sad fact of life. It may be that in a certain situation, I have injured someone (possibly a loved one) by speaking or acting in anger. But in a reflective moment, I may become remorseful and ask myself if I really want to be the kind of person (have the character of one) who does such things. If I do not want that, it will be necessary to change my thoughts and feelings. Just resolving not to do it again will be of little use. Will alone cannot carry us to change. But will *influenced through changing our thoughts and feelings* can result in our becoming the kind of people who just don't do that kind of thing anymore.

Remember that the will is what we're also calling the "heart" in this book. We're using *heart*, *will*, and *spirit* interchangeably but with slight shifts in emphasis to throw light on different aspects or functions of the heart.

As we've already seen, the thoughts and feelings that influence our will in any given moment cannot be changed *in* that moment. But following the VIM pattern can help us in our *future* choices. It is because of this fact that we are ultimately responsible for our character.

IDENTIFICATION OF OUR WILL WITH GOD'S WILL

What does a will look like that has been transformed into Christ-likeness? How is such a will characterized? Jesus said of himself (and, of course, he is always our pattern), "He who sent Me is with Me; He has not left Me alone, for I always do the things that are pleasing to Him" (John 8:29).

And Paul said this: "I have been crucified with Christ; and it is no longer I who live, but Christ lives in me; and the life which I now live in the flesh I live by faith in the Son of God, who loved me and gave Himself up for me" (Galatians 2:20).

We also recall John Calvin's words: "The only haven of safety is to have no other will, no other wisdom, than to follow the Lord wherever he leads. Let this, then, be the first step, to abandon ourselves, and devote the whole energy of our minds to the service of God."[1]

So now we have the answer to our question: *Single-minded and joyous devotion to God and his will—and to service to others because of him—is what the will transformed into Christlikeness looks like.* That is the outcome of Christian spiritual formation of the will, heart, or spirit. And this outcome becomes our *character* when it has become the governing response of every dimension of our being. Then we can truly be said to have "put on Christ" (Galatians 3:27, KJV).

THE BASIC NATURE OF THE WILL

As we've seen, the will (heart, spirit) is the core of who we are as individuals. It is in our will that we have a likeness to God or are "in his image." Another way to think about the will is that it is the source of our self-determination. Pure and absolute self-determination, of course, exists only in God. ("I AM *THAT* I AM,"

Exodus 3:14, KJV, emphasis added; compare John 5:26.) But will is limited, though still very real, in man. As we've already discussed, the primary exercise of the will in human beings is the power to select what we think about. From this decision, our other decisions and actions directly flow.

Character develops from our will as specific choices become habitual and, to some extent, automatic. Character is revealed most of all in what we feel and do without thinking. Character is also revealed in our remorse and repentance—in our sorrow over sin and our plea for God's help to break the patterns of habitual thinking and willing that move us in wrong directions.

WILL AND HUMAN DIGNITY

Why doesn't God just force us to do the things he knows to be right? It's because that would destroy precisely what he has intended in our creation: freely chosen character. Will is central to personhood, which is what makes the will dear to God and gives a human being *dignity*. Dignity is of such great worth that it doesn't allow exchanging human personhood for anything else.[2] The great worth of the person explains why Jesus Christ would die for the sake of individual human beings and be satisfied with the outcome (see Isaiah 53:11; Hebrews 12:2).

We treasure the will—the capacity for choice—in ourselves. Will has obvious, intrinsic, and supreme value. A small child, without *learning* to do so, values his capacity to act on his own, which he quickly identifies and stubbornly defends. The child's sense of things flowing from himself is unmistakably joyous and irrepressible. And adults delight to see the child's will emerge—"Look at what she did!" and "Did you hear what he said!" In the child and the adult, this sense of creativity is basic to health and well-being.

But the human will in the individual is not only precious; it is a problem. From the strictly human point of view, it is a devastating and unsolvable problem. We all have the experience of willing in a way that is contrary to earlier choices we have made or should have made. Human life is characterized by conflict within the will and among wills. But that statement is really too tame. What we call civilization is a smoldering heap of violence constantly on the verge of bursting into flame. That is the true picture of the fallen human will.

DUPLICITY, DECEITFULNESS, AND DARKNESS

Away from God, the constant condition of the will is *duplicity* and *fragmentation*. Many things are willed that cannot be reconciled with each other. Turned away from God, thoughts and feelings fall into chaos, and the will cannot help but follow.

The deceitfulness and darkness of the heart *apart* from God is inevitable to those who trust only themselves and so must try to take charge of their life. Jeremiah said,

> *The heart is devious above all else;*
> *it is perverse—*
> *who can understand it? (17:9, NRSV)*

And to answer that question, the prophet continued in the very next verse,

> *I the LORD test the mind*
> *and search the heart,*
> *to give to all according to their ways.* (NRSV)

To God, the duplicity of the human heart is totally transparent.

Very few of us could honestly say we are untouched in some way by our own duplicity. Few of us could say that we do not sometimes struggle to overcome deceit and darkness—within ourselves as well as around us.

Our only hope is to entirely place our confidence in the God and Father of Jesus Christ, who is willing to enter the duplicity of our heart and bring it wholly to himself as we earnestly invite him. He is *"greater than our heart* and knows all things" (1 John 3:20, emphasis added).

GOD HEARS THE HEART

The heart (will, spirit) is precisely what God observes and addresses in human beings. He cares little or nothing for outward show. He responds to the heart because it is, above all, who we are. It is who we choose to be. What God wants of us can come only from there. He respects the centrality of our will and will not override it. He seeks godly character in us to fulfill the eternal destiny he has in mind for us.

But God is sensitive to the slightest move of the heart toward him. This is the witness of both the Bible and of life. It doesn't matter whether you are "religious" or not ("Jew" or "Greek"), "for the same Lord is Lord of all, abounding in riches for all who call on Him; for 'WHOEVER WILL CALL ON THE NAME OF THE LORD WILL BE SAVED'" (Romans 10:12-13).

Multitudes of people have come to a full knowledge of God because in a moment of complete hopelessness, they prayed the Atheist's Prayer or something like it: "O God, if there is a God, save my soul, if I have a soul." When that is the true cry of the heart, of the inmost spirit, of the individual who no longer has any hope other than God, God hears and responds without fail. It is as if he has installed a "heart monitor" in every person. And when the heart truly reaches out to God *as* God, no longer looking to itself or others, he responds with the gift of "life from above."

In fact, God is constantly *looking* for people who will worship him "in spirit and in truth" (John 4:24, NIV). Who does that refer to? It refers to people who have freehearted and wholehearted admiration of, respect for, and commitment to God as the highest being of all. They never try to conceal anything from him and always rely completely on him.

And as for those whose heart is at its core completely given to him, who wholly rely on and hope in him, "The eyes of the LORD move to and fro throughout the earth that He may strongly support" them (2 Chronicles 16:9). And they can believe this promise:

The eyes of the LORD are toward the righteous,
And His ears are open to their cry. (Psalm 34:15)

From Surrender to Drama

In the progression toward complete identification of our will with God's, there are distinctions to be noted. First there is *surrender*. When we surrender our will to God, we consent to his supremacy in all things. Perhaps we do so grudgingly. We recognize his supremacy intellectually, and we concede to it in practice—though we still may not like it, and parts of us may still resist it.

We may not be able to do his will, but we are willing to will it. In this condition, there is still much grumbling and complaining about our life and about God. Andrew Murray comments that "we find the Christian life so difficult because we seek for God's blessing while we live in our own will. We should be glad to live the Christian life according to our own liking."[3]

But if grace and wisdom prevail in the life of the one who surrenders to God's will, he or she will move on to *abandonment*. Then the individual is *fully* surrendered. There is no longer any part of himself or herself that holds back from God's will. Typically, at the point of abandonment, surrender covers all the circumstances of life, not just the truth about God and his explicit will (the commandments).

While some things that happen to us may clearly not be what God would wish, he does allow everything—the tragic loss of a loved one or of health or opportunity, for example, or a grievous wrong done to us by others. We now accept these things as within God's plan for good to those who love him and are living in his purposes (see Romans 8:28). *Irredeemable* harm does not befall those who willingly live in the hand of God. What an astonishing reality!

Older Christian writers often speak of how we are privileged to "kiss the rod" of affliction that strikes us, even while trembling with weakness and pain. What a crucial lesson this is for spiritual transformation. We cease to live on edge, wondering, *Will God do what I want?* Pain will not turn to bitterness or disappointment to paralysis.

But there is still more. Beyond abandonment is *contentment* with the will of God, not only with his being who he is and ordaining what he has ordained, but also with the lot that has fallen to us. At this point in the progression toward complete identification with the will of God, gratitude and joy are the steady tones of our life. We are now *assured* that God has done well by us and will always do so—no matter what! Dreary, foot-dragging surrender to God looks like a far-distant country. Also, at this point duplicity looks like utter foolishness in which no sane person would be involved. Grumbling and complaining are gone (see Philippians 2:14-15)—not painstakingly resisted or eliminated but simply not considered. "Rejoice evermore" is natural and appropriate.

FROM ABANDONMENT TO CONTENTMENT — AND PARTICIPATION

But we are not done yet! Beyond contentment lies intelligent, energetic *participation* in accomplishing God's will in our world. We are no longer spectators but are caught up in a vivid and eternal drama in which we play an essential part. We embrace our imposed circumstances, no matter how tragic they seem, and act for the good in a power beyond ourselves. "We are reigning—exercising dominion—in life by One, Christ Jesus" (Romans 5:17, PAR), looking toward an eternity of reigning with God through ages of ages (see Revelation 22:5). We take action to accomplish the will of God in his power. We are carried along by the power of the divine drama within which we live actively engaged. So, far from struggling to resist sin, we are devoted to the realization of righteousness all around us. This is the real meaning of "Yet not I, but Christ liveth in me" (Galatians 2:20, KJV). The strongest human will is always the one that is surrendered to God's will and acts *with* it.

It may be that at present we cannot even imagine what it would be like for us to have a will significantly identified with God's will. But we must never forget that he "is able to do exceeding abundantly beyond all that we ask or think, in terms of the power that is working within us" (Ephesians 3:20, PAR; compare Isaiah 64:4). Our part is to begin as best we can.

"To Will One Thing"

When we set out on the path of the surrendered will, we find we must come to grips with our fallen character. This distorted character has taken over our habitual, or automatic, ways of thinking and feeling. It has shaped our past and present social world, permeated our body and its responses, and even sunk down into the unconscious depths of our soul. In their fallen nature, all the elements of our self position themselves against God.

The condition we find ourselves in can best be described as one of *entanglement*. By contrast, the condition we must move toward is that of single-minded focus upon doing the will of God in everything, distracted by nothing.

"Purity of heart," Kierkegaard said, "is to will one thing."[4] Before we can come to rest in such single-mindedness as the habitual orientation of all dimensions of our being, a serious battle is required. But the call of grace and wisdom is nonetheless to "lay aside every encumbrance and the sin which so easily entangles us, and . . . run with endurance the race that is set before us, fixing our eyes on Jesus" (Hebrews 12:1-2). We look to Christ's example of single-minded pursuit of God's will, even to the point of death.

"No soldier in active service entangles himself in the affairs of everyday life," Paul reminded Timothy, "so that he may please the one who enlisted him as a soldier" (2 Timothy 2:4). Dear Martha of Bethany was "worried and bothered about so many things," as Jesus pointed out, while only a few things were necessary—really only one: "Mary has chosen the good part, which shall not be taken away from her" (Luke 10:41-42). And Paul's own testimony was that he really did only one thing, which was to "press on toward the goal for the prize of the upward call of God in Christ Jesus" (Philippians 3:13-14).

THE ROLE OF SPIRITUAL DISCIPLINES

The person who intends to will what God wills begins with what God has *said* he wills. And we do not need to know *all* he has said. We can begin with what we know he has said. Let us firmly decide to do that. Who does not know, for example, that it is God's will that we should be without guile and malice? Then let us decide never to mislead people and never to do or say things merely to cause pain or harm. Let us decide that today, right now, we will not do such things. Lying and malice are foundational sins. They make possible and actual many other sins.

Of course when we begin to implement our decision, we discover that it is no simple task. We discover what a grip duplicity and malice have on us in every dimension of our being. Our thoughts and feelings and our usual routines of action have an influence over our choices that is much more powerful and complicated than we ever imagined. We discover that the mere intention or effort of will is not enough to bring about the change in us.

A major service of the spiritual disciplines is to cause the duplicity and malice that are buried in our will and character to surface and be dealt with. These disciplines might be solitude (being alone with God for long periods of time), fasting (learning freedom from food and how God directly nourishes us), worship (adoration of God, as discussed in chapter 6), and service (doing good for others with no thought of ourselves). Disciplines such as these make room for the Word and the Spirit to work in us, and they permit destructive feelings—feelings that are usually veiled by our standard practices and long-accepted rationalizations—to be uncovered and dealt with for what they are: our will, not God's will. Those feelings are normally clothed in layer upon layer of habitual self-deception and rationalization. Typically, they have enslaved the will. And the will, in turn, will have coerced the mind to conceal or rationalize what is really going on. Your mind will really "talk to you" when you begin to deny fulfillment of your desires, and you will find how subtle and shameless these destructive feelings are. I know this from experience.

Truly becoming one who wills above all to act with the kingdom of God and to have God's kind of goodness (see Matthew 6:33) will not happen overnight. But with a path of clear intention and decision, and with appropriate spiritual disciplines and accompanying grace to illumine and correct us when we fail, it is not as far away as we might suppose. The duplicities, entanglements, and evil intents that infect our will *can* be brought to light and eliminated as we keep our eyes on Jesus, who initiated and perfects our faith. For he is the One "who for the joy set before Him endured the cross, despising the shame, and has sat down at the right hand of the throne of God" (Hebrews 12:2).

SWEET WILL OF GOD

Do we then lose ourselves? To succeed in identifying our will with God's will is not, as is often mistakenly said, to have no will of our own. Far from it. To have no will is impossible. We would not even be a person. Rather, it is for the first time to have a will that is fully functional, not at war with itself. It will be capable of directing all the parts of our self in harmony with each other under the direction of God. Then we will not hesitate to do what is right.

In chapter 2, we noted that a person with a well-kept heart is *prepared for* and *capable of* responding to the situations of life in ways that are good and right. When through spiritual transformation we have come to know a measure of the well-kept heart in real life, we experience it as a gift of grace. This happens no matter how hard we may have struggled to grow into it. It is a gift through which we find, precisely, *ourselves*! This is just as Jesus taught: "He who has lost his life for My sake will find it" (Matthew 10:39).

For the first time, we not only have a fully functioning will, but we also have a clear identity in the eternal kingdom of God. Day by day we will have grace to make real this eternal kingdom in our life and in the lives of those near us. The will of God is not foreign to our will. It is sweetness, life, and strength to us. Our heart sings,

> *Sweet will of God,*
> *Oh, hold me closer,*
> *'Til I am wholly lost in Thee.*

Questions for Meditation and Response

1. How can you exercise your power to select what you think about?

2. What are some contradictory things that you will (or try to will)? For instance, maybe you want to express love to your spouse but also want to avoid being further drained at the end of a tiring day.

3. What do you try to get people to believe about you?

4. Identify an aspect of God's will that you're not yet able to do but that you're willing to will.

5. Meditate on this statement: *Irredeemable* harm does not befall those who willingly live in the hand of God. What's the evidence for or against this? Why should you believe it?

6. For the next week, try diligently not to mislead people nor to do or say anything merely to cause pain or harm. Notice times when you slip. At the end of each day, take stock of how you did. What do you learn from this exercise?

7. Or for the next week, choose one of your desires and systematically deny it. For instance, if you love meat, be a vegetarian. If you love to get places quickly, drive in the slow lane at the speed limit, stopping at yellow lights you would normally have sped through. If you like to work while you eat lunch, do nothing while you eat. What do you learn?

The Body, Our Primary Ally in Christlikeness

Are you unaware that your body is a shrine to the Holy Spirit from God, who is within you? And that you are not your own property? A price has been paid for you. So make your body a showplace of God's greatness.

1 CORINTHIANS 6:19-20, PAR

No longer present the parts of your body to sin as weapons of wickedness, but present yourselves to God like people who, coming out of death, have eternal life; and present your bodily parts to him as weapons of righteousness.

ROMANS 6:13, PAR

INCARNATION AND OUR PRESENT BODY

The way of Christ is relentlessly incarnational—it is *bodily*. Incarnation is not just a fact about Jesus, simply that "Christ is come in the flesh" (1 John 4:2, KJV). Rather, he came in a real human body so that he might bring redemption and deliverance to *our* body.

Our body is an essential part of who we are, and no redemption that omits it is full redemption. Those who deny that Christ has come in real flesh are antichrist, as John said (see 1 John 4:3).

Such a strong position is taken in the New Testament because redemption is for "the life which I now live in the flesh" (Galatians 2:20). This present life is caught up *now* in the eternal life of God. So my body must become holy—it must "come over" to Christ's side. Otherwise, my life as a whole could not "come over," and so it would be impossible that "as He is, so also are we in this world" (1 John 4:17).

Although the redemption of the body will be *completed* later, even now "if the Spirit of Him who raised Jesus from the dead dwells in you, He who raised Christ Jesus from the dead will also give life to your mortal bodies through His Spirit who dwells in you" (Romans 8:11). We are to know now "the power of His resurrection" (Philippians 3:10). Our body is not just a physical system but is inhabited by the real presence of Christ.[1]

Spiritual Formation of the Body

Spiritual formation requires the transformation of the body. The proper retraining and nurturing of the body is absolutely essential to Christlikeness. The body is not just a physical thing. As it matures, it increasingly takes on the quality of our "inner" life. (The body of a small child, by contrast, has almost no inner quality to it, which is why the child can really hide nothing.) In other words, the body increasingly becomes a major part of the hidden source *from which* our life immediately flows.

As we have seen, the outcome of spiritual formation is the transformation of the inner reality of the self in such a way that the deeds and words of Jesus become a natural expression of who we are. But it is the nature of the human being that the "inner reality of the self" settles into our body—becomes fused with it. Formed in sin, our character and our body are set against God and his ways, and as we look about us, we find our body running pretty much on its own—at least for a while.

When our heart (will, spirit) comes to new life in God, the old "programs" are still running contrary to our new heart, and for the most part they are running in our body and its parts or members. Paul said it this way: "Sin dwells within me . . . that is, in my flesh" (Romans 7:18, PAR). "Sinful passions" are still "at work in our bodily parts" (Romans 7:5, PAR), even though they no longer can "bring forth death." That is because our identity before God has been shifted over to another life that is in us as God's gift. While "the spirit is willing, but the flesh is weak" (Matthew 26:41), we may find ourselves doing the thing we hate (see Romans 7:15). But it really is no longer we who are doing it but the sin still functioning as a living force in the members of our body (see 7:23).

However, this is only a transitional state for those who can say with David, "My soul follows hard after you" (Psalm 63:8, PAR). The law or force of the Spirit of life that is in Christ Jesus is now also a real presence in our body, and it opens the way to liberation from the force of sin in our bodily parts (see Romans 7:23). By not walking in terms of the flesh but in terms of the Spirit, we are increasingly able to do the things that Jesus did and taught (see Romans 8:4). We move toward the place where both the spirit is willing and the flesh is strong for God because the Spirit now *occupies* our flesh. We have presented the members of our body "as slaves to righteousness, resulting in sanctification" (Romans 6:19).

WE MUST TAKE THIS LITERALLY

The various tendencies actually present in our bodily parts can *move* our body into action independently of our intentions to the contrary. Therefore, we act or speak before we think. The character that lives in our body carries us away.

Take the tongue, for example. James said that "the tongue is a small part [member, *mela*] of the body" (3:5). However, "the tongue is a fire, the cosmos of iniquity. The tongue is set among our members as something which defiles the entire body, setting fire to the natural course of things and is itself set on fire by hell" (3:6, PAR).

James had observed the incredible power of the tongue to stir up the inclinations of the whole body—our own body as well as that of others. Have you observed this? It is perhaps the last bodily part to submit to goodness and rightness. No one can tame it, James said. Physical violence nearly always is introduced by verbal violence.

It is only as we habitually subject the tongue to the grace of God as an instrument reserved for him to do his will that grace comes literally to inhabit and govern it. And when that happens, the effects spread throughout the body. "If anyone does not stumble in word," James said, "that is a perfect man, able even to guide his entire body aright" (3:2, PAR). "The tongue of the righteous is as choice silver" (Proverbs 10:20), and "A healing tongue is a tree of life" (Proverbs 15:4, PAR).

Other members of the body, though not as central to life as the tongue, have their own readiness to act wrongly:

> *Haughty eyes, a lying tongue,*
> *hands to shed innocent blood, . . .*
> *feet that run quickly to do evil. (Proverbs 6:17-18, PAR)*

The shoulders, the stomach, the genitals, the fists, and the face are constantly moving us away from God if they have not been permeated by the real presence of Christ.

A person caught up in rage or lust or resentment—or even religious self-righteousness—is one whose body has taken over. The body is totally running his or her actions, at least for the moment. Sometimes we say, "I just lost my temper." "Temper" refers to the capacity to handle all kinds of situations and maintain one's balance. It is close to *character*, as when we say that people are "acting out of character" or are "not themselves" today.

CHRIST DELIVERS US FROM BODY HATRED

Sincere people find evil at work in their bodies, and they wrongly blame the body for it. Throughout the ages, a burning sense of the powers of evil actually inhabiting our body—and specific parts—is one of the reasons *body hatred* has been such a dreadful fact.

People with this misguided and terribly harmful attitude toward the body correctly see the power of sin that really is in the body's parts. But they mistakenly assume that the evil *is* the body. They don't know how to think about the readiness to sin, the sinful intentions that have come to possess those parts through their adaptation to a world of sin. But it's important to realize the body itself is not evil.

Paul's teaching that we are to "present our bodily parts as servants to righteousness for sanctification" (Romans 6:19, PAR) stands in shocking opposition to the classical assumptions of his day. The same is true of his teaching that the body of the redeemed person is a shrine of the Holy Spirit: "The body is meant not for fornication but for the Lord, and the Lord for the body" (1 Corinthians 6:13, PAR). "Do you not know," he continued on to say, "that your bodies are members [*mela*] of Christ?" (6:15).

For most people today, our body runs our life. Contrary to the words of Jesus in Matthew 6:25, life is often *not* more than food nor the body more than clothing. Our time and energy are almost wholly devoted to how our body looks, smells, and feels. The body is used to meet ego needs such as admiration, sexual gratification, and power over others.

It is this bodily orientation of the self that runs the human cosmos, as the elderly apostle John pointed out: "For all that is in the world, the lust of the flesh and the lust of the eyes and the boastful pride of life, is not from the Father, but is from the world" (1 John 2:16). This is "the mind set on the flesh," Paul said, which is in opposition to "the mind set on the Spirit" (Romans 8:4-11).

THE ONLY REASONABLE USE OF OUR BODY

God owns our body. He is the one who gives it and takes it away (see Job 1:21). Our "reasonable service," therefore—the only thing that makes any sense for a human being who trusts Christ—is to "present our bodies as a living and holy sacrifice, very pleasing to God" (Romans 12:1, PAR). This total yielding of every part of our body to God, until the very tissues and muscles that make it up are inclined toward God and are vitalized in action by the powers of heaven, breaks all conformity with worldly life in this age. It transforms us into conformity with the age to come by completing the renewal of our mind—our powers of thought, imagination, and judgment, which are so deeply rooted in our body.

Freedom from the *thought* of evil—"thinketh no evil" (1 Corinthians 13:5, KJV)—requires that automatic responses toward evil no longer run our body. The bodily tendencies of the "living sacrifice" incline us away from evil.

TAKING STEPS

What are some things we can do to place our body fully in the redeeming power of God? Let's acknowledge once again that we need to make changes in the other dimensions of our person as well. Change in one area can't be successful in isolation from others.

Before looking at particular steps, let me mention two books that, though not widely known or available, are of great practical help in the spiritual formation of the body. The first is a little book

137

by Frances Ridley Havergal, *Kept for the Master's Use*. Many have sung her song "Take My Life, and Let It Be."[2] The fundamental spiritual attitude indicated in the words of that song is spelled out with remarkable intelligence and biblical force in her book.[3]

The second book is by Margaret Magdalen: *A Spiritual Check-up: Avoiding Mediocrity in the Christian Life*.[4] This fine treatment envisions each bodily part from the feet up as it enters the waters of baptism and explores what that should mean for the transformation of all our life in godliness. It is extremely helpful in thinking about the spiritual life of our body.

Now, in approaching the spiritual formation of our body, what should we do? There are a number of things:

1. We must actually release our body to God. That is what Paul means when he tells us "to present our body to God as a living sacrifice" (Romans 12:1, PAR). It needs to be a definite action, renewed at least on a yearly basis, if not more frequently.

Here's what I suggest: Realizing the importance of the body in spiritual formation, decide to give your body to God. Perhaps you can spend a day in silent and solitary retreat. Quiet your soul and your body; let them get clear of the fog of your daily burdens and preoccupations. Meditatively pray some central Scriptures before the Lord, especially those dealing with the body, such as those emphasized in this chapter.

I recommend that you lie on the floor, facedown or faceup, and explicitly and formally surrender your body to God. Then take time to go over the main parts of your body and do the same for each one. What you want to do is ask God to *take charge* of each part of your body—to fill it with his life and use it for his purposes.

Accentuate the positive; don't just think of not sinning with your body. Instead, actively consecrate it to God. Remember, a sacrifice is something *offered up* to God.

Give plenty of time to this ritual of sacrifice. Don't rush it. When you realize it's done, give God thanks, arise, and spend some time in praise. An ecstatic reading (chant and walk or dance) of Psalms 145–150 would be an excellent exercise. Put your *body* into it. Later, share what you have done with a spiritual friend or pastor and ask him or her to bless it. Review your ritual of sacrifice in thought and prayer from time to time over the following weeks and *plan* to renew the same ritual surrender at least once a year.

2. No longer idolize your body. What does that mean? It means that you no longer make it an object of "ultimate concern." You have, after all, given it up to God, and he can do with it as he wishes. You care for it only as it serves God's purposes in your life and in the lives of others. You don't worry about what will happen to it—sickness, repulsiveness, aging, death—for you have placed God in charge of all that. You freely take any issues that arise to him in prayer. You take good care of your body, but only within the framework of values clearly laid down by God and exemplified in Jesus Christ. You don't live in fear of your body and what it might do to you.

3. Closely allied with the above is that you do not misuse your body. This means primarily two things. First, you do not use it as a source of sensual gratification. Addictions of various kinds, such as inappropriate sensual gratification, are misuses of the body. Bodily pleasure is not in itself a bad thing. But when it is exalted to a necessity and we become dependent upon it, then we are slaves to our body and its feelings. Only misery lies ahead.

Second, this means that we do not use our body to dominate or control others. This means different things to different people. For example, we do not present our body in ways that elicit sexual thoughts, feelings, and actions from others. We do not try to be "sexy." We can be naturally attractive without that.

Another example has to do with intimidation by means of our body. There are many aspects of this, from subtle hints to brute force. The most common forms of it are social: "power dressing," sarcasm, and "knowing" looks and remarks. Having given up our body to God, we do not use it in these ways.

A final example is overwork. In our current world, this is a primary misuse of the body. It is said that work is the new "drug of choice." Often this can be excessive competition in some area of our common life. Or it can be a matter of wearing our body out in order to succeed. God long ago gave us these words: "It is vain for you to rise up early, to sit up late, to eat the bread of sorrows: for so he giveth his beloved sleep" (Psalm 127:2, KJV).

4. Now, the positive counterpart: The body is to be properly honored and cared for. The body must be regarded as holy because it is owned and inhabited by God. "The body is not for immorality, but for the Lord, and the Lord is for the body" (1 Corinthians 6:13). That being so, "Do you not know that your bodies are members of Christ?" (6:15).

But because our body is holy (separated to God), we must care for it through nourishment, exercise, and rest. The practical center of proper care for the body is Sabbath.

SABBATH REST

Sabbath fulfilled in human life is really celebration of God. Sabbath is inseparable from worship; genuine worship is Sabbath. As the fourth commandment, keeping the Sabbath is the fulfillment in practice of the first three. When we come to the place where we can joyously "do no work" (Leviticus 23:3, KJV), it will be because God is so exalted in our mind and body that we can trust him with our life and our world, and we can take our hands off them.

For most of us, Sabbath is first the practice of solitude and silence. We must carefully seek, cultivate, and dwell in these. When they become established in our soul and our body, we can practice them in company with others. But the body *must* be weaned away from its tendency to take control, to run the world, to achieve and produce, to attain gratification. Progress in the *opposite* direction can only be made in solitude and silence.

Rest is one primary condition of Sabbath in the body. If we really intend to submit our body as a living sacrifice to God, our first step may be to start *getting enough sleep.* Sleep is a good indicator of how thoroughly we trust in God.

The psalmist, who knew danger and uncertainty well, also slept well:

> *I lay down and slept;*
> *I awoke, for the LORD sustains me. (3:5-6)*

> *In peace I will both lie down and sleep,*
> *For You alone, O LORD, make me to dwell in safety. (4:8)*

Of course, we cannot just sleep our way to sainthood. Nor do we mean that godly people do not work hard or are never exhausted. But the saints who have separated their bodies to God have had resources not at the disposal of the ordinary person running on fumes and promises, where so many of us find ourselves today.

If we are not rested, the body moves to the center of our focus and makes its presence *more strongly* felt; the tendencies of its parts call out more strongly for gratification. Sensual desires have greater power over us through our body's desperation. Our awareness of what our body is doing—however subtly—and what is happening around us will be less apparent. Confusion is the enemy of sound spiritual orientation. Rest, properly taken, gives clarity to the mind. Weariness, by contrast, can make us seek gratification and energy from food or drugs, from various illicit relationships, or from egoistic postures that are, in Paul's words, "upon the earth" (Colossians 3:5, KJV). They pull us away from relying on God and from living in his power.

Much more could be said about the role of spiritual disciplines in the transformation of the body. For example, a full treatment would deal with how exercise and diet can ease the influence of the "sin that is in our members." You may wish to think these things through and ask for God's guidance during your retreat day of "ritual sacrifice."

Questions for Meditation and Response

1. Do you hate anything about your body? If so, what? How would God reply to these feelings?

2. In what ways are your time, energy, and money devoted to how your body looks, smells, and feels?

3. Meditate on Matthew 6:25. How easy is it for you to believe and do this? What gets in the way?

4. In what ways do you idolize your body? In what ways, if any, do you use it for sensual gratification or to control, manipulate, or intimidate others?

5. What should Sabbath rest look like in your life?

6. Do the exercise of releasing your body to God (see pages 138–139).

Chapter 10

Changing How We Relate to Others

The communities of God, to which Christ has become teacher and guide, are, in comparison with communities of the pagan people among whom they live as strangers, like heavenly lights in the world.

ORIGEN[1]

We know that we have passed out of death into life, because we love the brethren. He who does not love abides in death.

1 JOHN 3:14

TRUE SPIRITUAL FORMATION HAPPENS IN RELATION

Through his life and death, Jesus gave us a powerful directive for our spiritual formation: We must become people who love one another (see John 13:35). And Jesus does not allow "love" to be vague and unspecified. Instead, he gives us "a *new* commandment, that you love one another. *Just as I have loved you*, you also should love one another" (verse 34, NRSV, emphasis added). The age-old command to love is transformed—made a new command—by complete identification with the profound love Jesus has for us (see 1 John 2:7-8).

This supernatural love allows us to know that "we have passed out of death into life" (3:14). We simply can't love in *that* way unless we have a different kind of life in us. And this kind of love is identified with Christ *because* it is a love that makes us ready to "lay down our lives for one another" (3:16, NRSV).

Failure to love others as Jesus loves us chokes off the flow of the eternal kind of life that our whole human system cries out for. The old apostle minced no words: "He who does not love abides in death" (3:14). Notice that he did not say, "He who hates," but simply, "He who does not love." The mere absence of love is deadly. It is withdrawal from the life of God.

Our purpose, then, must be to become those who love others with Christ's *agape*. That purpose, when developed, will transform the social dimension of our self and all of our relationships. Love is not a special way of feeling.[2] Instead, it is the divine way of relating to others and to oneself that moves through every dimension of our being and begins to restructure our world for good.

GOD *IS* LOVE

This love is possible for each of us because of what God is. "God is Love." Yes, but we must not miss the essential point. The profound good news is not just that he *loves us*, as is often said. After all, even a mean person can love someone for special reasons (see Matthew 5:46-48). But more than this, God *is* Love. And he sustains his love *for us* from his basic reality as Love, which dictates his Trinitarian nature.

God is in himself a sweet society of love, with a first, second, and third person to complete a social matrix or "circle of sufficiency." In this circle, not only is there love and being loved between the Father and Son but also *shared* love for another, the Holy Spirit. Community is formed not by mere love and requited love, which by itself is exclusive, but by *shared* love for another, which is inclusive.

The nature of personality is inherently communal, and only the Trinity does justice to what personality is. We are told on the earliest pages of the Bible that "it is not good that the man should be alone," and so God decided to make "a helper to be a match for him" (Genesis 2:18, PAR). Centuries later, Paul pointed out that "not one of us lives unto himself and not one dies unto himself" (Romans 14:7, PAR). Further, Paul said, "Whether we live or die, we are the Lord's" (14:8). And for this purpose, "Christ died and lived again, that He might be Lord both of the dead and of the living" (14:9). Human beings are really *together only in God*, and all other ways of "being with" fall short of the needs of human nature. God completes the circles of sufficiency that are our human communities—beginning with the fundamental community of mother and child. The secret of all life-giving relations with others lies in the fact that *the primary "other" for a human being, whether he wants it or not, is always God.*

WHAT OUR RELATIONSHIPS COULD LOOK LIKE

Sin structures embedded in our soul and body have almost totally disabled us for those relationships with others that our heart longs for. So our purpose in spiritual formation is to hold up God's ideal and to seek it. Larry Crabb beautifully writes,

> *When two people connect, when their beings intersect as closely as two bodies during intercourse, something is poured out of one and into the other that has power to heal the soul of its deepest wounds and restore it to health. The one who receives experiences the joy of being healed. The one who gives knows the even greater joy of being used to heal. Something good is in the heart of each of God's children that is more powerful than everything bad. It's there, waiting to be released, to work its magic.*

Then Crabb adds, "But it rarely happens."[3] That is a sad fact of our time. The power of life in Christ is seldom realized today. But true spiritual formation, carried to fulfillment, would mean that what Crabb describes would *routinely* happen between his people. That is the meaning of the church as the body of Christ, the members nourishing one another with the transcendent power that raised up Christ from the dead and is now flowing through each member to the others.

THE REALITY OF REJECTION

In contrast to this vision, most people know a great deal about being rejected, being left out, or just not being welcomed or

148

accepted. As the parent/child relationship is perhaps the most perfect illustration of a circle of sufficiency in human life, so it is also the place where the deepest and most lasting wounds can be given. If in his early years, a child is totally received by his parents and siblings, he will very likely have a rootedness about him that will enable him to withstand most forms of rejection that often come upon a human being in a lifetime. He will carry his solid relationships to and from his family members throughout life, being sustained by them even long after those loved ones are dead.

By contrast, a small child *not* adequately received and loved can actually die. Or if he survives, he will likely be incapable of giving and receiving love in healthy human relationships for the rest of his life. He will be perpetually "left out," even if only in his imagination. The final words of the Old Testament speak of one who must come and "restore the hearts of the fathers to their children and the hearts of the children to their fathers" to avoid a curse coming to rest upon the land (Malachi 4:6).

Severe wounds to our rootedness in others may also occur later in life. Failures of various kinds, real or imagined, can bring rejection or detachment from parents and other significant figures. Unfaithfulness in a mate, divorce, failure in career advancement, collapse of a profession, disloyalty of children, or just never making it "in," wherever "in" may be[4]—all of these break up our human circles of sufficiency. They may leave us unconnected to others at levels of our soul where lack of nourishment from deep connections means spiritual starvation and loss of wholeness.

149

THE TWO BASIC FORMS OF EVIL IN RELATIONS WITH OTHERS

So when we come to deal with the spiritual formation of our social life, we have to start from our *woundedness*. It is hard to imagine anyone in this world who has not been deeply injured in his or her relationships. The exact nature of the poison of sin in our social dimension is fairly easy to describe, though extremely hard to deal with. It has two forms. They are so closely related that they really are two forms of the same thing: lovelessness, a lack of proper regard and care for others. These two forms are *assault*, or attack, and *withdrawal*, or distancing. They are so much a part of ordinary human existence that most people think they are just "reality" and never imagine that we could live without them.

If spiritual formation in Christ is to succeed, the power of these two forms of evil within our self absolutely *must* be broken. So far as it is possible, they must be eliminated as indwelling realities, as postures we take toward others. They also must be successfully disarmed as they come toward us from others. Perhaps we must be reconciled to the fact that they cannot be entirely eliminated from our world, or even from our fellowships of Christian believers, until a new epoch dawns. But we can eliminate them from our own being. We *can* live without them.

UNDERSTANDING ASSAULT AND WITHDRAWAL

We *assault* others when we act against what is good for them, even with their consent. It is not only when we harm them or cause them

150

pain against their conscious will. Hence, seduction is assault, as is participation in the social structures that institutionalize evil. The more explicit and well-known forms of assault are dealt with in the last six of the Ten Commandments—murder, adultery, theft, and so on. These are deepened in their meaning by the teachings of Jesus, especially in his Sermons on the Mount and on the Plain (see Matthew 5–7; Luke 6), and by the teachings of Paul in such passages as Colossians 3–4 and 1 Corinthians 13.

We *withdraw* from others when we regard their well-being as a matter of indifference to us; perhaps we go so far as to despise or hold contempt for them. We "don't care."

Both assault and withdrawal primarily involve our relations with those close to us. Clearly that means members of our family, those who live intimately with us, those with whom we work or play, and those with whom we share common goals or goods—our community.

UNDERSTANDING THE WRONGNESS

Assault surfaces early in the development of a child. It arises primarily from conflicts of desire. The child wants something that another child has. He does what he can to take that thing away from the other. But the other resists, and the children become angry with each other. Then they try to harm each other. This is the story of Cain.

Or perhaps people experience envy; perhaps one enjoys a status that the other does not. Feelings of resentment and contempt may arise and play back and forth between them. As we grow older, theft, lying, murder, adultery, and settled attitudes of covetousness fall into place. These are all forms of assault on others.

A verbal assault, whether refined or brutal (we speak of a "cutting remark"), is specifically designed to hurt a person and to inflict loss of standing or respect in his own eyes and before others. Many people never in their lifetime recover from a particular verbal assault or a pattern of assault.

But withdrawal within a relationship, like assault, also wounds those involved. And the tongue, once again, can assault by withdrawal—by not speaking. Some forms of withdrawal are motivated by weakness, fear, uncertainty, or even "gut reactions" toward how another person looks or acts.

Instead of being based on the evils of assault and withdrawal, our social life as God designed it is meant to be a play of constant mutual blessing. *Every* contact with another human being should be one of goodwill and respect with a *readiness* to acknowledge, make room for, or assist the other in suitable ways.

SPIRITUAL FORMATION IN MARRIAGE

To be married is to *give oneself to* another person in the most intimate and inclusive of human relationships, to support him or her for good in every way possible. This includes physically, emotionally, and spiritually, of course, but also with every conceivable dimension of his or her being. Nothing ever given to humanity more adequately portrays what *marriage* is than the traditional service known as the "Form of Solemnization of Matrimony," which appears in the old *Book of Common Prayer* of the Church of England.

Just consider some of its wording. Anyone who wishes to really understand the wreckage brought by divorce today should begin with careful study of the vows of this traditional service: "I . . . take thee . . . to have and to hold from this day forward, for better for worse, for richer for poorer, in sickness and in health, to love and to cherish, till death do us part. . . ." Insight into the meaning of these vows will clearly bring out *why* the ideal intent of marriage is one man and one woman for life. The "mutual submission to each other in awe of the Lord," which is the vision of marriage in Christ, eliminates both assault and withdrawal from this most basic of human relationships. Marriage provides the matrix or womb from which whole human beings can emerge to form whole human communities under God.

This "womb" is then, of course, the overall home life of the child, not just a particular part of the female body. Birth should be a move from one part to a larger part of the same home. This home is a community of constant sacrificial submission on the part of each for the good of the other. Where no children are involved, a man and a woman will still "lay down their life" for each other. That is the richly spiritual—and personally and relationally deepening—environment of marriage.

KEY ELEMENTS IN FORMING OUR SOCIAL DIMENSION

What will our transformed social life look like in our family, as well as in larger communities such as a local gathering of Christ's people? Let's look at four key elements of the new world of redeemed relationships.

Receiving God's Vision of Our Wholeness in Him

The *first* element in the transformed social dimension is for individuals to come to see themselves as *whole*, as God himself sees them. Such a vision sets them beyond the wounds and limitations they have received in their past relationships with others. It is this vision of oneself from God's point of view that makes it possible to regard oneself as blessed, no matter what has happened. "We are dead," Paul tells us, and "our life is hid with Christ in God. When Christ, who is our life, shall appear, then we will appear with him, glorious" (Colossians 3:3-4, PAR). We have stepped into a new life where the primary relationship is with Christ, and we are assured of a glorious existence forever.

God has a plan for each of us in the work he is doing during our lifetime, and no one can prevent this from being fulfilled if we place our hope entirely in him. The part we play in his plans now will extend to the role he has set before us for eternity. Our life in him is whole and blessed, *no matter what has or has not been done to us, no matter how shamefully our human circles of sufficiency have been violated.*

It is God's sufficiency to us that secures everything else. Again, Paul said, "Our sufficiency is of God" (2 Corinthians 3:5; 9:8, PAR). It is the God-given vision of ourselves as whole in him that draws all the poisons out of our relationships and enables us to go forward with sincere forgiveness and blessing toward others. Only in this way can we stand free from the wounds of the past and from those who have assaulted or forsaken us.

DEFENSIVENESS GONE

The *second* element in the spiritually transformed social dimension is abandonment of all defensiveness. Of course, this can occur only in a social context where Christ dwells—that is, among his special people. But it will naturally occur in the absence of attack and withdrawal, wherever that place of relative peace may be.

Abandonment of defensiveness calls for a willingness to be known for who we really are in our most intimate relationships. It includes abandonment of all efforts at self-justification, evasiveness, deceit, and manipulation. That is not to say we should impose all the facts about ourselves upon those close to us, much less on others at large. Of course we shouldn't do that (though we may want to find a friend with whom we can confess our private sins, as James 5:16 urges). But it does mean that we should not hide, that we should not attempt to "look good."

Jesus' teachings about not performing for public approval and not being a hypocrite—having a face that differs from our reality—find application here (see Matthew 5–6).

GENUINE LOVE PREDOMINATES IN OUR GATHERINGS

The *third* element in our transformed social dimension is the banishing of all pretence. Love between Christians would then "be genuine," as Paul instructed the Romans. That is the focal point in the beautiful picture of local gatherings Paul gives us in Romans 12:1-21. Christ's apprentices would be carrying out their particular work in the group life with a grace and power that is not from themselves but from God (see verses 3-8). Each one would be exhibiting the following qualities (see verses 9-21):

1. Letting love be completely real
2. Abhorring what is evil
3. Clinging to what is good
4. Being devoted to one another in familial love *(philostorgoi)*
5. Outdoing one another in giving honor
6. Serving the Lord with ardent spirit and all diligence
7. Rejoicing in hope
8. Being patient in troubles
9. Being devoted constantly to prayer
10. Contributing to the needs of the saints
11. Pursuing (running after) hospitality
12. Blessing persecutors and not cursing them
13. Rejoicing with those who rejoice and sorrowing with those in sorrow
14. Living in harmony with each other
15. Not being haughty but fitting right in with the "lowly"
16. Not seeing themselves as wise
17. Never repaying evil for evil
18. Having due regard for what everyone understands to be right
19. Being at peace with everyone, so far as it depends on them
20. Never taking revenge, but leaving that to God
21. Providing for needy enemies
22. Not being overwhelmed by evil, but returning good instead

This is the most adequate biblical description of what a spiritually transformed social dimension looks like. Just think what it would be like to be part of a group of disciples in which this list was the conscious, shared *intention* and where it was actually lived out. It would totally transform the marriage relation and family. Its effect on the community would be incalculable, as it has been wherever it's been realized among Christ's people.

To achieve this in our social dimension, we must have heard and accepted the gospel of grace, of Jesus' defenseless death on the cross on our behalf. We must revel in his acceptance of us and stand safe and solid in his kingdom.

The *fourth* element is an opening up of our broader social life to God's work in the world. Without the burden of having to defend ourselves, we can devote our life to the service of others. Our social relations are set before us as an infinite task, which can be carried out only in the power of God. We do not even know how to pray as we ought, Paul tells us, but we have the Spirit who "intercedes for us with groanings too deep for words" (Romans 8:26). This is true community, the fruit of our transformed social life.

Questions for Meditation and Response

1. Meditate on the truth that God's basic reality is Love.

2. Describe in detail some times when you've experienced completeness in a circle of relationships or some times when you've experienced broken relationships.

3. Describe an experience of assault or withdrawal that wounded you.

4. Describe a time when you wounded someone else through assault or withdrawal. If you can't think of a time, consult Matthew 5–7 or 1 Corinthians 13 for ideas.

5. Journal about a vision of yourself that is beyond the wounds and limitations you have received in past relationships. Write about yourself as God sees you: whole and blessed, no matter what has happened in the past. Matthew 5:2-12 or Isaiah 49:13-21 might be of help here.

6. How would your relationships be affected if you saw yourself as whole in God?

Chapter 11

Transforming the Soul

Only give heed to yourself and keep your soul diligently, so that you do not forget the things which your eyes have seen.

DEUTERONOMY 4:9

"Take My yoke upon you and learn from Me, for I am gentle and humble in heart, and YOU WILL FIND REST FOR YOUR SOULS."

MATTHEW 11:29 (SEE ALSO JEREMIAH 6:16)

At this moment, the dimension of you that is running your life is your soul. Not external circumstances, not your thoughts, not your intentions, not even your feelings, but your soul. The soul is that aspect of your whole being that *correlates*, *integrates*, and *enlivens* everything going on in the various dimensions of your self. It is the life center of the human being. It regulates whatever is occurring in each dimension and how it interacts with the others. The soul is "deep" in the sense of being foundational and also in the sense that it lies almost totally beyond conscious awareness.[1]

In the person with a "well-kept heart," the soul is properly ordered under God and in harmony with reality. The outcome is a person who is *prepared for* and *capable of* responding to the situations of life in ways that are good and right.

THE PSALM 1 PERSON

That is how it is with the man in Psalm 1. He does not determine his course of action by what those without God say—even in their latest brilliant ideas. That is, he does not live as if God does not exist, nor does he make plans from within a strictly human understanding. He "does not walk in the counsel of the wicked" but in the counsel of God (verse 1).

The Psalm 1 man *delights* in the law of God (see verse 2). He loves God's law, is thrilled by it, and can't keep his mind off of it. He thinks it is beautiful, strong, wise, and an incredible gift of God's mercy and grace. He therefore dwells upon it day and night, turning it over and over in his mind and speaking it to himself.

The result is a flourishing life. The image used here is that of a tree planted by water canals. No matter what the weather or the surface condition of the ground, its roots go down into the water sources and bring up life. As a result, it bears fruit when it is supposed to, and its foliage is always bright with life. It prospers in what it does. The same is true for the man who is rooted in God through his law: "In whatever he does, he prospers" (verse 3; compare Joshua 1:8).

THE POWER OF WORD AND SPIRIT

The soul's formation—the character it has taken on through its life course—is seen in the details of how thoughts, feelings, social relations, bodily behaviors, and choices unfold and especially how they interact with each other. In most cases, individuals are not at harmony with themselves, much less with the truth of God. Their habitual condition is one of conflict. They often act contrary to how they themselves intend.

But we must not underestimate the soul's power of recovery when in touch with the Word and Spirit of God. Robert Wise observes, "Reconnected to the Spirit of God, lost souls discover they have power and capacity beyond anything they could have dreamed. The restoration of soul is more than a recovery of connectedness. Significant strength, ability to achieve, guidance, and awareness are imparted."[2]

Truly we are "fearfully and wonderfully made" (Psalm 139:14). The human soul is a vast spiritual (nonphysical) landscape with resources and relationships that exceed human comprehension. We know only that God is over all and that the soul, if it can only acknowledge its wounded condition, manifests amazing capacities for recovery when it receives God's grace.[3]

THE INNER STREAM

Our soul is like an inner stream of water, which gives strength, direction, and harmony to every other element of our life. When that stream is as it should be, we are constantly refreshed and exuberant in all we do because our soul itself is deeply rooted in the vastness of God and his kingdom. All else within us is enlivened and directed by that stream.

Beyond the image or picture of an inner stream is this reality:

Life is self-initiating, self-directing, self-sustaining power. In this full sense, of course, *only God has life.* That is the biblical view. Moreover, in his "hand is the soul of every living thing," Job tells us (12:10, PAR). "The Father has life in Himself," Jesus taught, and "gave to the Son also to have life in Himself" (John 5:26). "He alone possesses undying life," according to Paul (1 Timothy 6:16, PAR), and is the one "who gives and preserves life to all things" (verse 13, PAR).

The human being receives its *relatively* "self-initiating, self-directing, self-sustaining power" from the hand of God. The human soul utterly depends on its unique spiritual relationship with God for its very life—whether it is aware of this dependence or not (see Genesis 2:7). Therefore, when we speak of the human soul, we are speaking of the *deepest level of life and power* in the human being.

GOD HAS A SOUL

Many people are surprised to learn that God, too, has a soul. Even translators of the Bible often do not seem to know what to do about it. Referring to the gross wickedness of Judea, the prophet Jeremiah gives the Lord's word: "Be thou instructed, O Jerusalem, lest my soul depart from thee; lest I make thee desolate, a land not inhabited" (Jeremiah 6:8, KJV). But more recent versions translate this as "or I shall turn from you in disgust" (NRSV) or "or I shall be alienated from you."

A similar situation occurs in Jeremiah 9:9: "Shall not my soul be avenged on such a nation as this?" (KJV); "Shall I not bring retribution on a nation such as this?" (NRSV); and "On a nation such as this shall I not avenge Myself?"

In these and other cases, the word *nephesh* (or *soul*) occurs in the Hebrew texts with reference to God. That is done in order to indicate the utter depth of the response of God to the wickedness of his people. That depth is not successfully communicated by the alternative language offered. The true meaning is hollowed out and lost. Similar observations must be made about Isaiah 1:14 (where KJV and NRSV, but not NASB, use "soul"). In speaking of the *soul* of God, reference is always made to the deepest, most fundamental level of his being. References to God's soul can be found in other places in the Bible as well, such as Leviticus 26:11, Psalm 11:5, and Matthew 12:18, which says, "BEHOLD, MY SERVANT WHOM I HAVE CHOSEN; MY BELOVED IN WHOM MY SOUL IS WELL-PLEASED."

The heart of the matter is that to refer to someone's soul is to say something about the ultimate depths of his or her being—something that cannot be communicated with terms such as "person" or "self" (see Matthew 11:29; Luke 12:19).

APPLIED TO THE HUMAN SOUL: BIBLICAL CASES

If you take this idea of the deepest and most fundamental level of a life and apply it to biblical references to the *human* soul, you will see that it makes great sense of what the Scripture is saying. Human life has many aspects that are superficial, not the real essence of life. They are not *soul*.

We could look at many passages in both the Old and New Testaments, but let's consider Jesus' teaching that it does not profit one to gain the whole world and lose his or her own soul (see Matthew 16:26). We might ask, What does it mean to lose our soul?

What it means is that our whole life is no longer under the direction of our inner stream of life because it has been taken over by exteriors. The rich farmer who said, "Soul, you have many goods laid up for many years to come; take your ease, eat, drink and be merry" (Luke 12:19), is an example of this. He abandoned his soul in favor of externals. He laid up treasure for himself but was not "rich toward God" (verse 21). On the positive side, we see Mary calling upon her soul—that is, the deepest part of her being—to "magnify the Lord" (Luke 1:46, KJV). James spoke of how the engrafted word "is able to save your souls" (1:21). Paul and his coworkers strengthened "the souls of the disciples" as they returned through the cities of Asia Minor (Acts 14:22), and he spoke to the Thessalonians of how they not only gave them the gospel of God but also imparted "our own souls" (1 Thessalonians 2:8, KJV). Peter spoke of disciples purifying their souls in obedience (1 Peter 1:22).

THE CRIES OF THE SOUL

Once we clearly acknowledge the soul, we can learn to hear its cries. Jesus heard its cries from the wearied humanity he saw around him. He saw the soul's desperate need in those who struggled with the overwhelming tasks of their life. Such weariness and endless labor was, to him, a sure sign of a soul not properly rooted in God—a soul, in effect, on its own. He saw the multitudes around him, and it tore his heart, for they were "distressed and dispirited like sheep without a shepherd" (Matthew 9:36). And he invited such people to come and become his students ("learn of me," Matthew 11:29, KJV) by yoking themselves to him—that is, letting him show them how he would pull their load.

Jesus' own greatness of soul showed itself in meekness and lowliness (see Philippians 2:3-11). Being in his yoke is not a matter of taking on additional labor to crush us all the more but rather of learning how to use his strength *and* ours together to bear our load *and* his. We will find his yoke an easy one and his burden a light one because in learning from him, we will find rest for our soul. Our soul is at peace only when it is with God, as a child with its mother.

ABANDONING OUTCOMES

What we most learn in Jesus' yoke, beyond acting with him, is to abandon *outcomes* to God. In doing this, we accept that we do not have within ourselves—in our own "heart, soul, mind, and strength"—the wherewithal to make *anything* we do come out right. Even if we "suffer according to the will of God," we must simply "entrust [our] souls to a faithful Creator in doing what is right" (1 Peter 4:19). This is a major part of the meekness and lowliness of heart that we learn in his yoke. And what rest comes with it!

Humility is the framework within which all virtue lives. Angela of Foligno observed, "One of the signs by which a man may know that he is in a state of grace is this—that he is never puffed up."[4]

Accordingly, we are to "clothe [ourselves] with humility," Peter said (1 Peter 5:5), which certainly means loss of self-sufficiency. "GOD . . . GIVES GRACE TO THE HUMBLE," he continued. "Therefore humble yourselves under the mighty hand of God, that He may exalt you at the proper time, casting all your anxiety on Him, because He cares for you" (verses 5-7). Humility is the great secret of rest for the soul because it does not presume to manipulate outcomes.

We simply have to rest in God's life as he gives it to us. Because of the Christ revealed in the Bible, we know that God is good. Therefore, we can cast outcomes on him. We also find experience of this rest while we labor in the yoke of Christ. Resting in God, we can be free from all anxiety, which means deep soul rest. Whatever our circumstance, taught by Christ we are enabled to "rest [be still] in the LORD and wait patiently [or longingly] for Him" (Psalm 37:7). We don't fret or get angry because others seem to be doing better than we are, even though we may feel they are less deserving than we are.

"THE LAW OF THE LORD IS PERFECT, CONVERTING THE SOUL"

The written law that God gave to the Israelites is one of the greatest gifts of grace God has ever conveyed to the human race. It is part of the blessings God promised would come to all the families or nations of the earth through Abraham and his seed. Of course, there is much more to the law than just rules or commandments. It provides a picture of reality—of how things are with God and his creation. The Prophets and the Gospels share with "the Law" this vital function of enabling human beings to know God—to know what God is doing and what we are to do. For in that knowledge lies our true well-being.

Therefore, Moses challenged his people, "For what great nation is there that has a god so near to it as is the LORD our God whenever we call on Him? Or what great nation is there that has statutes and judgments as righteous as this whole law which I am setting before you today?" (Deuteronomy 4:7-8).

The law of the Lord gratefully received, studied, and internalized to the point of obedience is "perfect," as Psalm 19:7 says. There is nothing lacking in it for its intended purpose. It therefore converts or restores the soul of those who seek it and receive it. It is a living and powerful being, capable of distinguishing soul from spirit in man and dealing with them appropriately and redemptively (see Hebrews 4:12).

Nothing in the Old Testament suggests that what the law does in the human heart is a human accomplishment. Rather, all benefit is ascribed to the law itself and to its giver. (You may want to study Psalm 119 carefully.) The benefit of the law would be a loss if we viewed it as something we must achieve on our own. For in attempting to *use* the law in this way, we will throw ourselves back into the position of self-idolatry, attempting to exploit the law as a tool for managing ourselves and God.

This mistake is what led to the horrible degradation of "the Law" at the time of Jesus and Paul. It became a pathway away from grace toward an instrument of cultural self-righteousness and social oppression. "Woe to you lawyers!" Jesus said, "For you have taken away the key of knowledge. You did not enter in yourselves, and those who were entering in you hindered" (Luke 11:52, NKJV).

"HE RESTORETH MY SOUL"

It is always true—from the beginning of the Bible to the end—that human deliverance comes from a personal relationship with God, established through God's gracious love and power. *But the law is an essential part of that relationship.* The inadequacy of human effort alone is simply assumed. Still, the law was given as an essential meeting place between God and human beings in covenant relationship with him. The law is where the sincere heart would be received, instructed, and enabled by God to walk in his ways. God is the only restorer of souls. When those who walk in personal relationship with him take his law into their heart, that law quickens and restores connection and order to their flagging souls. But that enlivening never happens in the absence of the personal presence and gracious action of God.

Thus some of the greatest assurances of God's personal presence are found in the Old Testament, for example in the book of Isaiah:

> *"Do not fear, for I am with you;*
> *Do not anxiously look about you, for I am your*
>   *God.*
> *I will strengthen you, surely I will help you,*

> *Surely I will uphold you with My righteous right*
> *   hand. . . .*
> *I will open rivers on the bare heights*
> *And springs in the midst of the valleys;*
> *I will make the wilderness a pool of water*
> *And the dry land fountains of water. . . .*
> *That they may see and recognize,*
> *And consider and gain insight as well,*
> *That the hand of the LORD has done this,*
> *And the Holy One of Israel has created it."*
>
> *   (41:10,18,20)*

Spirit, covenant, and law always go hand in hand within the path of spiritual formation, for that is the path of one who walks with God.

LAW AND GRACE GO TOGETHER

Everything in the Scriptures goes against spurning the law. Jesus himself identified those who love him as the ones who keep his commandments (see John 14:23-24). John said bluntly, "Sin is lawlessness" (1 John 3:4). Paul, equally bluntly, wrote, "Abstain from every form of evil" (1 Thessalonians 5:22). And Jesus said, "Why do you call Me, 'Lord, Lord,' and do not do what I say?" (Luke 6:46). Paul made a major point of explaining that

> *what the law could not do [namely, secure human*
> *conformity to itself by its own power] because of the*

weakness of human abilities, God brought about by sending his own Son in the likeness of sinful flesh, and by condemning sin in the flesh [showing it up for the imposter it is, on its own turf], in order that what the law requires might be fulfilled in us, who do not walk in terms of the flesh, but in terms of the spirit. (Romans 8:3-4, PAR)

The presence of the Spirit and his grace is not meant to set the law aside but to enable conformity to it from an inwardly transformed personality. We walk in the spirit of the law, and the letter naturally follows. We cannot separate spirit from law, though we must separate spirit *and* law from *legalism*—righteousness in terms of actions.

The law *by itself* kills off any hope of righteousness through human effort, but it fans the flame of hope in God ever brighter as we walk in the law through "Christ in [us], the hope of glory" (Colossians 1:27). Grace does not set law aside except on the one point of justification—that is, acceptance before God. To the contrary, law is a primary instrument of spiritual transformation in union with "the spirit of life in Christ Jesus."

INNER AFFINITY BETWEEN LAW AND SOUL

There is an inner affinity between the law and the soul. That is why rebellion against the law makes the soul sick and distances it from God. That is why love of the law restores the soul. Law is good for the soul. It is an indispensable instrument of instruction and a standard of judgment of good and evil. Walking in the law with God restores the soul because the law expresses the order of God's kingdom and of God's own character. That is why it converts and restores the soul. Grace is also essential, but not grace as formless spurts of permissiveness that thrust the law aside.

The correct order that the soul requires for its vitality is found in the "royal law" of love (James 2:8), abundantly spelled out by Jesus and his teaching. That law includes all that was essential in the older law, which Christ fulfilled and enables us to fulfill through constant discipleship to him. One whose aim is obedience to the law of God in the Spirit and power of Jesus will have a soul at rest in God. And that soul will advance steadily and significantly in spiritual transformation into Christlikeness.

Questions for Meditation and Response

1. How would you explain what a soul is?

2. What would a Psalm 1 person look like in your home or workplace?

3. Meditate on Matthew 16:26. What does it mean to lose your soul? Think of someone who has gained a lot of money but has lost his or her soul in this life or someone who has been taken over by exteriors and isn't directed by an inner stream of life. What behaviors does a loss of soul produce?

4. Meditate on a psalm of God's goodness and greatness, such as Psalm 104.

5. Meditate on Exodus 20:1-17. How is God's law good for your soul in particular?

6. Write a prayer to God in which you abandon to him the outcome of some current desire. What thoughts and feelings go with this decision?

Being the Light of the World

*You were formerly darkness, but now you are light
in the Lord; walk as children of light (for the fruit
of light consists in all goodness and righteousness
and truth), verifying what is pleasing to the Lord.*

THE APOSTLE PAUL, EPHESIANS 5:8-10, PAR

*The simple program of Christ for winning the
whole world is to make each person he touches
magnetic enough with love to draw others.*

FRANK LAUBACH[1]

GOD'S GREAT PURPOSE

God's great purpose for humanity, as set forth in the Bible, is to
bring forth an immense community of people from "every nation
and tribe and tongue and people" to worship him (Revelation 14:6).
This great congregation of men and women will be a kingdom of
priests under God (see Revelation 1:6; 5:10; Exodus 19:6) who for
some period of time in the future will actually govern the earth
under him (see Revelation 5:10). Beyond that, they will also reign
with him in the eternal future of the cosmos, forever and ever (see
Revelation 22:5).

Brought together as a living community, these people will form a special dwelling place for God. It will allow his magnificence to be known and gratefully accepted by all of creation through all ages (see Ephesians 2:7; 3:10; Philippians 2:9-11). What the human heart now vaguely senses *should* be, eventually *will* be, in the cosmic triumph of Christ and his people. And those who have fully taken on the character of Christ—those "children of light" in Paul's language (Ephesians 5:8; 1 Thessalonians 5:5)—will be empowered by God in eternity to do what they want as free, creative agents. And what they do will always harmonize perfectly with God's own purposes.

Spiritual formation in Christlikeness during our life here on earth is a constant movement toward this eternal appointment God placed upon each of us in our creation—"the kingdom prepared for you from the foundation of the world" (Matthew 25:34). This movement forward is now carried on through our apprenticeship to Jesus Christ. It is a process of character transformation toward complete trustworthiness before God.

A COMPOSITE PICTURE OF "CHILDREN OF LIGHT"

Let's draw together our prior studies of the person who is being spiritually formed to create a composite picture of "the children of light." To call them *children* of light is to say that they have the basic nature of light: Light is their parent and has passed on to them its nature, as any parent does.

These people are not perfect, nor do they live in a perfect world—at least, not yet. But they are remarkably changed. Their

174

difference is not a pose they strike or things they do or don't do, though their behavior has become very different and distinctive. Where the children of light differ is primarily and most importantly on the "inside." It lies in their depths.

Thought life. Perhaps the first thing that comes to our attention when we get to know their inner life is what is on their mind. Quite simply, they think about God. He is never out of their mind. They love to dwell upon God and upon his greatness and loveliness, as brought to light in Jesus Christ. They adore him in nature, in history, in his Son, and in his saints. One could even say they are "God-intoxicated" (see Acts 2:13; Ephesians 5:18), though no one has a stronger sense of reality and practicality than they do. Their mind is filled with biblical expressions of God's nature, his actions, and his plans for them in his world. They do not dwell upon evil. It is not a big thing in their thoughts. They are sure of its defeat, and they deal with it appropriately in specific situations.

Because their mind is centered upon God, all other good things are also welcome there. "Whatever is true, whatever is honorable, whatever is right, whatever is pure, whatever is lovely, whatever is of good repute, if there is any excellence and if anything worthy of praise," their mind ponders those things (Philippians 4:8). They are positive, realistically so, based upon the nature of God as they understand it.

Feelings. And then perhaps we notice that the emotional life of these children of light is deeply characterized by love. That is how they invest the emotional side of their being. They love lots of good things, and they love people. They love their life and who they are. They are thankful for their life—even though it may contain many difficulties, even persecution and martyrdom (see Matthew 5:10-12). They receive all of it as God's gift, or at least as his allowance. Joy and peace are also with them even in the hardest of times—even when suffering unjustly. Because of what they have learned about God, they are confident and hopeful and do not indulge thoughts of rejection, failure, and hopelessness, because *they know better*.

Heart (will, spirit). Looking a little deeper, we find that these children of light really are devoted in their heart to doing what is good and right. Their will is habitually attuned to good, just as their mind and emotions are habitually homing in on God. They are attentive to rightness, to kindness, and to helpfulness, and they are purposefully knowledgeable about life, about what people need, and about how to do what is right and good in appropriate ways.

These are people who do not think first of themselves and what they want. They really care very little about getting their own way. They follow Paul's instruction to "regard one another as more important than yourselves; do not merely look out for your own personal interests, but also for the interests of others" (Philippians 2:3-4). These are easy and good words to them. Children of light are abandoned to God's will and do not struggle and deliberate as to whether they will do what they know to be wrong. They do not hesitate to do what they know to be right.

Body. What is right, of course, involves their body. Their body has come over to the side of their will to do good. It is constantly *poised* to do what is right and good without thinking. It is no longer true of them that their "spirit is willing, but the

176

flesh is weak" (Matthew 26:41). They know by experience that these words of Jesus are not a declaration about the inevitable condition of humans but a diagnosis of a condition to be corrected. The Spirit has substantially taken over their "members."

Consequently, we do not see them always being trapped by what their tongue, facial expressions, eyes, hands, and so forth have *already* done before they can think—for their body and its parts are consecrated to serve God and are habituated to be his holy instruments. They instinctively avoid the paths of temptation. The bodies of these people even *look* different. There is a freshness about them, a kind of quiet strength, and a transparency. They are rested and playful in a bodily strength that is from God. He who raised up Christ Jesus from the dead has given life to their bodies through his Spirit that dwells in them.

Social relations. In their relations with others, they are completely transparent. Because they walk in goodness, they have no use for darkness, and they achieve real connection or fellowship with others—especially other apprentices of Jesus. "If we walk in the Light as He Himself is in the Light, we have fellowship with one another, and the blood of Jesus His Son cleanses us from all sin" (1 John 1:7). And "The one who loves his brother abides in the light and there is no cause of offence in him" (2:10, PAR). They do not conceal their thoughts and feelings (nor do they impose them upon everyone). Because of their confidence in God, they do not try to manipulate and manage others. They do not go on the attack or on the hunt, intending to use or to hurt others.

Moreover, they are completely noncondemning, while at the same time they will not participate in evil. They pay evil only the attention absolutely required in any social setting. Beyond that, patient and joyful nonparticipation is their rule. They know how to truly *be present* with others without sharing in evil, as was true of Jesus himself. Of course, as was the case with Jesus, others may disapprove of their being in certain situations or with certain people, and there are always *some* occasions when they just step away. But they do not reject or distance themselves from the people who may be involved in such situations. They know how to "love the sinner and hate the sin" gracefully and effectively.

Soul. Finally, although those who know only the human powers of the flesh will *never* be able to understand these children of light (see 1 Corinthians 2:14), light nevertheless glows from within them. It is not just on the surface. It is deep, and in a certain obvious sense, it is effortless. It *flows*. That is, the things we have been describing in preceding chapters are not things the children of light are constantly trying hard to do, gritting their teeth and carrying on. Instead, these are features of life that well up out of a soul that is at home in God.

This is the outcome of spiritual formation in Christlikeness. It doesn't mean perfection, of course, but it does mean a person whose soul is whole: a person who has experienced a revolution of character.

THE SPIRITUAL GROWTH PROGRESSION
AS LAID OUT BY PETER

Is there a progression that spiritual formation typically follows? The apostle Peter gives us biblical insight into this process in

2 Peter 1:3-11. Starting from the bedrock of "God's divine power, that has granted to us everything pertaining to life and godliness," the apostle proceeds to point to the "precious and magnificent promises" of God that make it possible for us to "become partakers of the divine nature, having escaped the corruption that is in the world through excessive desire or lust" (verses 3-4, PAR).

And how is this escape to come about? By putting forth *our very best efforts*—"applying all diligence," a good translation says—to add to our faith (our confidence in Christ) moral excellence or *virtue*. That is, to train ourselves to do what is good and right. Notice this is something *we* must do; it will not be done for us.

And then, to our virtue, we must add knowledge or *understanding*. That is, we must come to know why the good and right we do *is* good and right and operate from insight into the realities of it all.

And then, to our insight, add *self-control*. That is, develop the capacity to carry out our intentions and not be thrown off by any turn of events.

And then, to our self-control, add *perseverance* (endurance, patience). This is the capacity to stick with the course, to stay with it over the long haul, regardless of how we may feel.

And then, to our perseverance, add *godliness*. Perhaps we can best think of this as depth and thoroughness of all the preceding attainments of grace. God is characterized by his inexhaustible resources of goodness.

And then, to our godliness, add the *kindness* and *gentleness of care*, which one sees among siblings and true friends. The word here is *philadelphia*. That is, extend family feeling and action to those in our community. Just think what that would mean to this wounded world. But it is possible to do this superhuman thing only through the goodness and strength of godliness.

And then, to our brotherly kindness, add *agape* love. This is the kind of love that characterizes God himself and is spelled out in heartrending detail on the cross of Jesus and in 1 Corinthians 13. It goes far beyond *philadelphia* and into the very heart of God. We are not just to love as family, but as he loved us (see John 13:34). *Agape* love is always presented, in the biblical descriptions of the children of light, as the ultimate move, which completes and solidifies all the other gains in spiritual progression (see Romans 5:5; 1 Corinthians 13; Galatians 5:14; Ephesians 4:15-16; Colossians 3:14; 1 John 4:16).

Peter concludes his great progression by telling us that if we do what he says here, we will "never stumble" and that "entrance into the eternal kingdom of our Lord and Savior Jesus Christ will be *abundantly* supplied to you" (2 Peter 1:10-11, emphasis added).

Understanding Sanctification

And now we can begin to speak of sanctification as a condition of the human soul established in imparted (not just imputed) righteousness. It is the condition of soul in the mature children of light. Sanctification requires *both God's effort and ours*. But what exactly is sanctification? This concept used to be much better understood than it is now, so we will turn to some older authors. In his *Systematic Theology*, A. H. Strong quotes the famous New Testament scholar Godet:

The work of Jesus in the world is twofold. It is a work accomplished for us, destined to effect reconciliation between God and man; it is a work accomplished in us, with the object of effecting our sanctification. By the one a right relation is established between God and us; by the other, the fruit of the reestablished order is secured. By the former, the condemned sinner is received into the state of grace; by the latter the pardoned sinner is associated with the life of God.[2]

Strong goes on to quote a striking illustration from another, unknown author: "The steamship whose machinery is broken may be brought into port and made fast to the dock. She is *safe*, but not *sound*. Repairs may last a long time. Christ designs to make us both safe and sound. Justification gives the first—safety; sanctification gives the second—soundness."[3]

A. A. Hodge speaks of the inseparability of accepting Christ's forgiveness and accepting his sanctifying work: "Any man who thinks he is a Christian, and that he has accepted Christ for justification, when he did not at the same time accept him for sanctification, is miserably deluded in that very experience."[4] Strong adds these vital comments: "Not culture, but crucifixion, is what the Holy Spirit prescribes for the natural man. . . . The Holy Spirit enables the Christian, through increasing faith, more fully and consciously to appropriate Christ, and thus progressively to make conquest of the remaining sinfulness of his nature."[5]

An excellent contemporary writer, Wayne Grudem, opens his discussion of sanctification by speaking of

> *a part of the application of redemption that is a progressive work that continues throughout our earthly lives. It is also a work in which God and man cooperate, each playing distinct roles. This part of the application of redemption is called sanctification: Sanctification is a progressive work of God and man that makes us more and more free from sin and like Christ in our actual lives.*[6]

So what shall we say about sanctification in summary? It is a consciously chosen and sustained relationship of interaction between the Lord and his apprentice. The apprentice is increasingly able to do what he or she knows to be right before God because all aspects of his or her person have been substantially transformed.

THE LIGHT OF THE WORLD

Jesus walked among humanity as the light of the world (see John 8:12; 9:5). What did that mean? "In Him was life," the apostle John said, "and the life was the Light of men"—a light of such power that the darkness in the world could not extinguish it (John 1:4-5). Light means both energy and knowledge. From the person of Christ there uniquely came into the world the energy and knowledge by which human beings could be delivered from evil and enabled to live life as it ought to be lived.

This is why Jesus sent out his disciples to make apprentices of all ethnic groups on earth. What he had in mind was *worldwide moral revolution — a revolution of character*. That would call for the population of the earth — or at least a substantial minority — to be transformed into "the children of light." Ordinary human beings in their ordinary positions in life would be appointed and empowered by him to be "the light of the world." It would no more be possible to hide them than it is possible to hide a city set on a hill (see Matthew 5:14-16).

NOW IS THE TIME TO *BE* CHILDREN OF LIGHT

That is where we now stand in our world — within earshot of the continuing call of Christ to take part in a revolution of character. We are beyond the point where *mere talk* can make an impression. Demonstration is required. We must live what we talk, even in places where we cannot talk what we live. If the bewildering array of spiritualities and ideologies that throng our times really can do what apprenticeship to Christ can do, what more is there to say?

There is no effectual response to our current situation except for the children of light to *be* who they were called to be by Christ, their head. Only when those who know that Jesus Christ is the light of the world take up their stand with him and fulfill their calling from him to *be* children of light where they are will there be any realistic hope of stemming the tide of evil.

The call of Christ today is the same as it was when he left us here to serve him "even to the end of the age" (Matthew 28:20). That call is to be his apprentices, alive in the power of God, learning to do all he said to do, leading others into apprenticeship to him, and also teaching them how to do everything he said.

If we follow *that* call today in our Christian groups, then, as in past times, we will once again see among us the presence of the God who answers by fire. We will be able to say as Moses said to the Lord long ago, "Is it not by Your going with us, so that we, I and Your people, may be distinguished from all the other people who are upon the face of the earth?" (Exodus 33:16).

Questions for Meditation and Response

Consider planning a half or full day of silent retreat for this final reflection.

1. Reflect once again on the vision of what you can be like as an apprentice of Jesus. Meditate on one or more of the following passages and note habits of thought, feeling, will, body (behavior and speech), social relations, and soul. Write down phrases and why they seem especially significant. You might walk and ponder a phrase.

   • Matthew 5–7
   • Romans 12
   • 1 Corinthians 13
   • 2 Corinthians 3:12–7:1
   • Galatians 5:22–6:10
   • Ephesians 4:20–6:20
   • Philippians 2:3-16; 4:4-9

- Colossians 3:1–4:6
- 1 Peter 2:1–3:16
- 2 Peter 1:2-10
- 1 John 4:7-21

2. How do you respond to the idea that you can actually become like this? Do you read these passages with longing, guilt, hopelessness, hope, excitement? Why?

3. What will it take for you to become like this?

4. Counting the cost of pursuing—or not pursuing—this as your life's priority, what is your settled intention? Tell God and at least one trusted person soon.

5. What will be your next step(s)?

6. What help do you need?

Afterword

The Christian life is a life of joy. This is not a lonely race we run, for we run *with* our Teacher. We keep looking up at Jesus, who gives us faith to run and who will bring us safely to the end (see Hebrews 12:2). We concentrate on his thoughts, feelings, character, body, social bearing, and soul. We constantly learn from him, and he shows us how to let the entanglements, weights, and sins drop off so that we can run more effectively.

As we run, we sense the Holy Spirit's divine assistance making our steps lighter. We realize truth more strongly and see things more clearly. We find greater joy in those running with us—our companions in Christ and those who went before and are coming after. His yoke *is* easy, we find. His burden *is* light. As our "outer self" perishes, our "inner self" is renewed on a daily basis (see 2 Corinthians 4:16). And no matter what the difficulty, we sing as we run, "Deliverance will come!"

But this is not a race of constant activity. It must have times of pausing—times of retreat, solitude, and prayer. Sometimes it is wise to do specific planning. Individually, we must ask ourselves what the particular things are that we need to do in order to bring the triumph of Christ's life more fully into the various dimensions of our being. Are there areas where our will is not abandoned to God's will or where old segments of fallen character remain unchallenged? Do some of our thoughts, images, or patterns of thinking show more of our kingdom or the kingdom of evil than they do of God's kingdom? For example, what are our habits as they relate to money or social practices or efforts to bring the world to Christ? Is our body still our master in some area?

And if we have some role in leadership among Christ's people, are we doing all we reasonably can to aid and direct their progress in inward transformation into Christlikeness? Is that progress the true aim of our life together, and are there ways in which our activities might be more supportive of that aim? Is the teaching that goes out from us appropriate to the condition of the people, and is our example one that gives clear assurance and direction? Is our "progress evident to all" (1 Timothy 4:15, PAR)?

Whatever our situation is, now is the time to make the changes and undertake the initiatives that are indicated in this book. Spiritual formation in Christlikeness is the sure outcome of well-directed action that is under the personal supervision of Christ and is sustained by his grace. This aching world is waiting for the people explicitly identified with Christ to be, through and through, the people he intends them to be. This is the case whether the world realizes it or not. There is no other hope on earth.

And that, of course, is where we stand: *on earth*. Strangely, perhaps, it is only spiritual formation in Christ that makes us at home on earth. We are pilgrims, and we look for a better city (see Hebrews 11:16). But we are content that this is not yet. Christ brings us to the place where we are able to walk beside our neighbors, whoever they may be. We are not above them. We are beside them as their servants, living with them through the events common to all of us.

We are not called to judge our neighbors but to serve them as best we can by the light we have, humbly and patiently with the strength God supplies. If it is true that our ways will at some point part for eternity, we shall love them none the less for it. And the best gift *we* can give them is always *the character and power of Christ in us and in others who really trust him.* Beyond this, we look to God for the revolution of their character as well.

Notes

Chapter 1: A Revolution Has Begun

1. In the midst of much misunderstanding about Jesus, the historian Will Durant still correctly grasped the role of Jesus as world revolutionary: "He is not concerned to attack existing economic or political institutions. . . . The revolution he sought was a far deeper one, without which reforms could only be superficial and transitory. If he could cleanse the human heart of selfish desire, cruelty, and lust, utopia would come of itself, and all those institutions that rise out of human greed and violence, and the consequent need for law, would disappear. Since this would be the profoundest of all revolutions, beside which all others would be mere *coups d'etat* of class ousting class and exploiting in its turn, Christ was in this spiritual sense the greatest revolutionist in history." Will Durant, *Caesar and Christ* (New York: Simon & Schuster, 1944), 566.

2. Although we do not intend a scholarly treatment in this book, it may be helpful to compare such statements about spiritual formation and spirituality to some other authors, for example Richard P. McBrien, *Lives of the Saints* (San Francisco:

HarperSanFrancisco, 2001), especially 18–19, and Francis A. Schaeffer, *True Spirituality* (Wheaton, IL: Tyndale, 1971), especially 16–17. An understanding of many deep problems concerning spirituality and spiritual formation can be gained by comparing these and other authors with what I say in this book.

3. Please see chapter 5 of my book *The Divine Conspiracy* (San Francisco: HarperSanFrancisco, 1998) for a more detailed explanation of Jesus' teachings on these and related matters.

4. The well-known hymn from which these lines were taken, "Rock of Ages" by Augustus Toplady, captures what has been the understanding of Christ's people through most of their past: that Christian redemption involves, in seamless unity, both the remission of guilt for sins and the deliverance of our lives from domination by sin. Though these are *distinct*, they were not, in our past, generally thought of as *separable*, and of course they aren't separable—ever. Recall also the words of Charles Wesley's hymn "O for a Thousand Tongues": "He breaks the power of canceled sin, / He sets the pris'ner free; / His blood can make the foulest clean; / His blood availed for me."

CHAPTER 2: THE HEART, CENTER OF OUR LIFE

1. On this and on points immediately following concerning the body and its role in the spiritual life, see my book *The Spirit*

of the Disciplines (San Francisco: HarperSanFrancisco, 1988), chapters 5–7.

Chapter 3: A Magnificent Ruin

1. C. S. Lewis, *The Weight of Glory* (Grand Rapids, MI: Eerdmans, 1973), 15.

2. Philip Yancey, "Lessons from Rock Bottom," *Christianity Today,* July 10, 2000, 72. It is one of the all-time greatest ironies of human history that the founding insights and practices of the most successful recovery program ever known—insights and practices almost 100 percent borrowed from bright spots in the Christian movement, if not outright gifts of God—are not routinely taught and practiced by churches. What possible justification or explanation could there be for this fact?

3. John Calvin, *Institutes of the Christian Religion*, vol. 2 (Grand Rapids, MI: Eerdmans, 1975), 7.

4. Calvin, 9.

Chapter 4: Restoration of the Soul

1. John Calvin, *Institutes of the Christian Religion*, vol. 2 (Grand Rapids, MI: Eerdmans, 1975), 7.

2. For a study of the deep roots of Calvin's spirituality in the Christian past, see Lucien Joseph Richard, *The Spirituality of John Calvin* (Atlanta: John Knox Press, 1974).

3. Calvin, 7.

4. See Calvin, chapter 7, book 3.

5. Saint Francis of Assisi, *The Little Flowers, The Mirror of Perfection, and the Life of Saint Francis*, ed. Thomas Okey (London: J. M. Dent, 1950), 15–16.

6. For further discussion of the roots and centrality of anger in life apart from God, see chapter 5 of my book *The Divine Conspiracy* (San Francisco: HarperSanFrancisco, 1998).

CHAPTER 5: CHRIST'S PATTERN FOR SPIRITUAL TRANSFORMATION

1. For development of this concept, please see chapters 1–2 of my book *The Divine Conspiracy* (San Francisco: HarperSanFrancisco, 1998).

2. In his "On the Improvement of the Understanding," the Jewish philosopher Spinoza (1632–1677) wrote of his decision "to inquire whether there might be some real good having power

to communicate itself, which would affect the mind singly, to the exclusion of all else: whether, in fact, there might be anything of which the discovery and attainment would enable me to enjoy continuous, supreme, and unending happiness." This is the universal human desideratum for all who think and have not in some measure despaired.

3. Adequate treatment of inner hindrances and positive steps against them used to be fairly standard among Christian teachers. As a case in point, see the many writings of Richard Baxter (died 1691).

CHAPTER 6: THE BATTLE FOR OUR THOUGHT LIFE

1. A. W. Tozer, *The Knowledge of the Holy* (New York: Harper and Brothers, 1961), 10. See also A. W. Tozer, *Worship: The Missing Jewel* (Harrisburg, PA: Christian Publications, 1992).

2. Roland H. Bainton, *Here I Stand: A Life of Martin Luther* (New York: The New American Library, 1955), 144.

3. To understand these matters further, see J. P. Moreland, *Love Your God with All Your Mind* (Colorado Springs, CO: NavPress, 1997), and James W. Sire, *Habits of the Mind: Intellectual Life As a Christian Calling* (Downers Grove, IL: InterVarsity, 2000).

4. Thomas Watson, *All Things for Good*, rev. ed. (1663; repr., Carlisle, PA: The Banner of Truth Trust, 1986), 74.

5. One of the best places to begin understanding what disciplines are and how they work is Richard Foster's *Celebration of Discipline: The Path to Spiritual Growth* (San Francisco: HarperSanFrancisco, 1978, 1998). This understanding is absolutely crucial to the renovation of the heart. It is a primary part of the *means* in the VIM structure.

6. To come to know many of these people of the past, study Richard Foster's *Streams of Living Water* (San Francisco: HarperSanFrancisco, 1998), and James Gilchrist Lawson's *Deeper Experiences of Famous Christians* (Uhrichsville, OH: Barbour, 2000).

Chapter 7: Educating Our Feelings

1. Jeff Imbach's *The River Within* (Colorado Springs, CO: NavPress, 1998) is very helpful in clearing up the importance of feeling to human life and spirituality.

Chapter 8: Transforming Our Character

1. John Calvin, *Institutes of the Christian Religion*, vol. 2 (Grand Rapids, MI: Eerdmans, 1975), 7.

2. Kant is still the best expositor of this point. See his *Foundations of the Metaphysics of Morals*, section 2 (many editions), as well as his other writings in ethics.

3. Andrew Murray, *Absolute Surrender* (Chicago: Moody, n.d.), 124.

4. Søren Kierkegaard, *Purity of Heart Is to Will One Thing: Spiritual Preparation for the Office of Confession* (New York: Harper, 1956).

CHAPTER 9: THE BODY, OUR PRIMARY ALLY IN CHRISTLIKENESS

1. Disagreements about the nature of the body abound in the fields of health care and medicine today. For an older but very illuminating treatment of the body, see Walter B. Cannon, *The Wisdom of the Body* (New York: Norton, 1932), as well as, more recently, Philip Yancey and Paul Brand's *Fearfully and Wonderfully Made* (Grand Rapids, MI: Zondervan, 1997).

2. This can be found, for example, as number 335 in *Worship and Service Hymnal* (Chicago: Hope Publishing Company, 1957), and in many other standard hymnals.

3. Frances Ridley Havergal, *Kept for the Master's Use* (London: James Nisbet & Company, Ltd., 1897).

4. Margaret Magdalen, *A Spiritual Check-up: Avoiding Mediocrity in the Christian Life* (East Sussex, UK: Highland Books, 1990).

CHAPTER 10: CHANGING HOW WE RELATE TO OTHERS

1. Origen, *Against Celsus*, III, 29, quoted in John Hardon, *The Catholic Catechism* (Garden City, NJ: Doubleday, 1975), 215.

2. The finest exposition of the biblical and moral concept of love I know of is in Charles Finney, *Lectures on Systematic Theology* (Grand Rapids, MI: Eerdmans, 1953), lectures 12–15. In particular, Finney strongly shows that love is not a *feeling*.

Today in "Western culture," there are two broadly different ways of thinking about love. Hardly anyone today rejects love as some kind of ultimate value and guide to life. But to most people, to love someone now means to be prepared to approve of his desires and decisions and to help him fulfill them. "If you love me, you'll do what I want" is the cry here. In the biblical (and any sane) view, to love someone means to favor *what is good for him* and to be prepared to help him toward that, even if that means disapproving of his desires and decisions and attempting, as appropriate, to prevent their fulfillment.

A serious problem is created today by the identification of the *good* and the *desired*. If there is no point of reference for good other than desire, then the identification (confusion) of these two things naturally follows. And there is then no way to distinguish the desired from the desir*able*. Of course from the biblical point of view, we have ample resources for distinguishing them.

3. Larry Crabb, *Connecting* (Nashville: Word, 1997), xi.

4. See C. S. Lewis's discussion of "The Inner Ring" and the desire to be in it as "one of the great permanent mainsprings of human action." *The Weight of Glory* (Grand Rapids, MI: Eerdmans, 1973), 61.

CHAPTER 11: TRANSFORMING THE SOUL

1. The one thing most approaches to the human being take for granted is that there is *something* "deep" in it, from depth psychology to deep structures of myth and language. Some of the popular writers of our time really never give any other idea of the soul other than that it is "deep."

2. Robert L. Wise, *Quest for the Soul* (Nashville: Nelson, 1996), 88.

3. One of the most realistic and instructive testimonies of the soul's response to grace in tragedy is Jerry Sittser's *A Grace Disguised: How the Soul Grows Through Loss* (Grand Rapids, MI: Zondervan, 1995). The final pages, 178–181, say pretty much all that needs to be said on this point.

4. Ann Stafford, "Angela of Foligno," in *Spirituality Through the Centuries: Ascetics and Mystics of the Western Church*, James Walsh, ed. (New York: P. J. Kenedy & Sons, n.d.), 191.

CHAPTER 12: BEING THE LIGHT OF THE WORLD

1. Frank Laubach, *Man of Prayer* (Syracuse, NY: Laubach Literacy International, 1990), 154.

2. Godet, quoted in Augustus H. Strong, *Systematic Theology*, rev. ed. (1907; repr., Valley Forge, PA: Judson Press, 1993), 869.

3. Quoted in Strong, 869.

4. A. A. Hodge, quoted in Strong, 869.

5. Strong, 870.

6. Wayne Grudem, *Systematic Theology: An Introduction to Biblical Doctrine* (Grand Rapids, MI: Zondervan, 1994), 746. See the remainder of Grudem's helpful discussion in the following pages.

About the Authors

Dallas Willard is a professor and former director of the School of Philosophy at the University of Southern California. He received his PhD from the University of Wisconsin. Dallas is the author of more than thirty publications, including *The Divine Conspiracy*, *The Spirit of the Disciplines* (both HarperSanFrancisco), and *Hearing God* (InterVarsity). He and his wife, Jane, live in Chatsworth, California. They have two children and one grandchild. Many of his writings in philosophy and religion are available from his web page, www.dwillard.org.

Don Simpson is currently the senior developmental editor for NavPress. He also participated in launching *Discipleship Journal* and *The Small Group Letter* and was cofounder of Helmers & Howard, Publishers. Don and his wife, Becky, live in Colorado Springs. They have two grown children.

TAKE A PERSONAL SPIRITUAL RETREAT.

The Pursuit of Holiness (25th Anniversary Edition)

Holiness should mark the life of every Christian, but it's often hard to understand. Learn what holiness is and how to say no to the things that hinder it.

Jerry Bridges   1-57683-463-8

Love Your God with All Your Mind

Have you really thought about your faith? This book examines the role of reason in faith, helping you use your intellect to further God's kingdom.

J. P. Moreland   1-57683-016-0

Renovation of the Heart: An Interactive Student Edition

With easy-to-understand examples, review questions, and explanations of keywords, this book will help you learn how to understand one of the most complicated and important lessons of life: putting on the character of Christ.

Dallas Willard and Randy Frazee   1-57683-730-0

To order copies, visit your local Christian bookstore,
call NavPress at 1-800-366-7788, or log on to www.navpress.com.

To locate a Christian bookstore near you,
call 1-800-991-7747.

NAVPRESS ®
BRINGING TRUTH TO LIFE
www.navpress.com